The XXL Vegan
Cookbook

Quick and Delicious Recipes for Every Day incl. Side Dishes and Desserts

Sarah Harrison

ISBN - 9798511573571

TABLE OF CONTENTS

MAIN COURSES 55

INTRODUCTION

What is a vegan lifestyle?

Veganism is a lifestyle that excludes the use of animal products. For many vegans, this can encompass diet, clothing, shoes, cosmetics and many other products too. Vegans do not eat meat, fish, eggs, dairy, honey, bee pollen or anything that is derived from an animal source.

As well as cutting out animal products from your diet, if you are transitioning to a fully vegan lifestyle this also means eliminating the use of any types of products that have come from an animal-based source from your daily life. For example, vegans generally do not wear leather and do not use cosmetics that contain animal derivatives. It can also mean ensuring that your products are cruelty-free and have not been tested on animals.

When it comes to adopting a vegan lifestyle, it can be important to check whether or not there are hidden animal products in your foods or cosmetics. For example, some varieties of wine are clarified using isinglass, which is obtained from fish.

Of course, veganism can be much more complex than a simple one-size-fits-all approach. When it comes to diet, there are a variety of different ways of eating within veganism. There is an array of different types of vegan diets such as:

- Raw-food vegan diet – based on the consumption of fruits and veggies, nuts and other plant-based foods that are uncooked and served below 48 degrees Celsius.

- Mock-food vegan diet – based on foods that mimic meats and other animal products without actually containing animal products.

- Whole-food vegan diet – based on eating fruits, vegetables and whole grains.

> ⮝ Fruitarian diet – based on eating mostly raw fruits and green foods and keeps the consumption of fatty foods to a minimum.

Many vegans do not just concentrate on their diets but also exclude the use of leather, suede, wool and other animal-based clothing from their lifestyle too. They opt for products that are cruelty-free and have not been tested on animals.

If you are considering following a vegan lifestyle, you can be as rigid or as flexible as you choose. To transition to a vegan lifestyle, you can do so gradually, by starting to introduce more vegan meals into your diet before making a complete transition.

In this book, you will find a varied range of meals that can help you to start to live your life in a more vegan way. Whether you are just embarking on a vegan journey or if you are already a committed vegan, these recipes are specifically designed to appeal to anyone who wants to live a healthy and cruelty-free lifestyle without sacrificing delicious and varied foods.

Naturally Vegan Foods

Although there are many "mock" foods available on the market, such as false meats that are designed to taste like the real thing, there is a myriad of readily available healthy and tasty foods that are naturally vegan. By increasing your consumption of these foods, you can boost your health and ensure that your diet is giving you all the essential nutrition that your body requires.

Fruit and vegetables:

Fruits and vegetables are nature's source of nutrients. Many experts encourage eating a rainbow diet. This means that you should try to incorporate a variety of differently coloured foods into your daily regime. Eating greens, reds, yellows and oranges ensures that you are getting a variety of essential vitamins and minerals and looking after your health.

Fruits and veggies contain nutrients such as:

- Iron – essential for the healthy functioning of your blood.

- Calcium – necessary for strong bones, teeth, nerves and muscles and a resilient immune system.

- Magnesium – crucial for strong bones and the regulation of blood pressure.

- Potassium – also helps to maintain healthy blood pressure.

- Vitamin A – important for your eyes and vision.

- Vitamin C – essential for teeth, gums and the ability that the body has to heal from injuries.

- Folate – necessary for the production of red and white blood cells and essential in pregnancy to prevent foetal defects.

- Sodium – helps bodily cells to function correctly.

Grains

Grains are an excellent way to get your necessary sources of many vitamins and minerals and they give you the crucial energy that you need to function on a daily basis. Whole grains, such as quinoa and amaranth are often rich in iron, and B-vitamins.

What's more, if you consume more grains in your diet you will also increase your fibre consumption which is necessary for a healthy digestive system.

Legumes

Lentils, peas, peanuts and beans are a few examples of legumes. They are rich in energy and nutrients and are often a great way to add a little extra protein to a meal. They are popular "bulking" foods in many countries around the world. That is to say, as they are generally relatively inexpensive foods, they can be used to produce a more satisfying meal whilst simultaneously keeping costs down.

Nuts and Seeds

Nuts and seeds, especially those that have their skins on or are in their natural, unprocessed form, are an important source of many minerals. For example, you can find nutrients such as zinc, magnesium, iron and selenium in many varieties of nuts. Seeds are an excellent source of omega-3 and protein too, ensuring that your vegan diet is not lacking in any crucial nutrients.

Vegetable Oils

Oils can be a rich source of healthy fats. Coconut oil, olive oil and rapeseed oil are all great for use in cooking or as a base for dressings and vinaigrettes.

Non-dairy milk

One of the benefits of non-dairy milk is that they are often fortified with calcium and vitamin D to ensure that vegans can benefit from the same nutrients as non-vegans. This will help to keep your bones and teeth healthy as well as facilitating the normal functioning of your immune system, muscles and nerves.

"Veganuary"

A vegan diet is an integral part of life for many people but it does not have to be rigid. You can choose the type of vegan diet that works for you and adapts to your lifestyle. Veganuary is the perfect example of how veganism can work on a part-time basis for many people.

If you are not familiar with Veganuary, it takes place every year in January. Those who take part in it commit to being vegan for one month to gain the health benefits of a vegan diet. For the rest of the year, you can eat your regular diet or become a "part-time" vegan, eating a vegan diet one or two days per week.

Of course, if you are just starting to transition to a vegan diet, then you can try this out during any month of the year. To embark on a vegan journey, try introducing one vegan meal per day and then gradually increasing your consumption of vegan foods. Snack on fruits, vegetables and nuts as this will not only help your transition to veganism but will also ensure that you are getting a range of essential nutrients that will help you to improve your health and wellbeing.

Many people who participate in "Veganuary" enjoy it so much that they make it an integral part of their regular lifestyle. However, it is important to remember that when you go vegan, you do not have to be rigid. Your individual needs are personal to you. Therefore, if you want to be a "flexitarian" and only eat a vegan diet sometimes, then there is nothing wrong with that. It is your choice and you can find the most suitable and appropriate way to eat that suits your requirements.

In general, changing to a vegan diet either on a flexible basis or a full-time basis can make you more mindful about the overall choices that you make about your meals. It can help you to opt for healthier options as well as incorporate considerations about a sustainable lifestyle into your daily routine, allowing you to feel better, look better and ensure that your personal choices have a positive ecological impact on the world around you.

Benefit One: It can help you to lose weight

Studies have shown that vegans tend to have a lower Body Mass Index (BMI) than non-vegans. This is because vegan diets are often lower in calories than other kinds of diets. Therefore, switching to a plant-based diet is an excellent way to shed some of those pounds and achieve a healthy weight.

However, it is not simply about the calorie count. The overall basis for a vegan diet and the way that it is constructed may also contribute to the weight loss that many people experience when they eat a vegan diet. For example, an increased intake of fibre and whole foods can make you feel fuller for longer, thereby decreasing the chances that you will snack on unhealthy foods.

Benefit Two: Vegan diets tend to be higher in fibre

More fruit, vegetables and grains equate to a higher fibre intake. Fibre is essential for the body because it helps to maintain a healthy gut and digestive system. Without it, you may experience horrible constipation and even related health problems, such a bowel cancer. By eating a healthy and balanced vegan diet, you may reduce the chances of colon cancer because you are increasing your intake of fibre.

Benefit Three: Your intake of fruit and veggies is likely to be higher

Fruits and vegetables are nature's gifts to us. They are jam-packed full of the essential nutrients that are crucial to good physical and mental health. As plant-based diets often centre around fruits and vegetables, then switching to a vegan diet will naturally encourage you to eat more of these types of foods.

The UK government recommends eating at least five portions of different fruits and vegetables every single day. However, many people struggle with incorporating that amount of fruit and veg into their regime. With a vegan diet, it is a lot easier because so many meals naturally encompass a selection of nutrient-rich fruits or vegetables.

Benefit Four: Vegan diets are linked to a lower risk of heart disease

A vegan diet could boost your heart health and your cardiovascular system could substantially benefit from a vegan diet. Studies have shown that plant-based diets are linked with a lower incidence of heart disease. There may be many reasons for this, including the significantly lower intake of saturated fat that is associated with a vegan diet.

Additionally, as vegan diets are rich in a variety of vitamins and minerals that promote heart health, this could also help to ensure that your heart and circulatory system maintain an optimum condition. Importantly, vegan diets have been linked with lowering cholesterol which also gives many benefits when it comes to maintaining a healthy cardiovascular system.

Benefit Five: A vegan diet could reduce the risks of certain cancers

Studies have shown that eating fewer animal products and more plant-based foods can lower the chances of being diagnosed with cancer. Plants produce a variety of phytochemicals that are associated with helping the human body to reduce inflammation and protect cells from sustaining damage. Therefore, there have been links between plant-based diets and lowered risks of certain cancers.

What is more, the nutrients that are found in plants, such as fruits and vegetables, are essential for good health and this overall boost to health may help to contribute to this lowered risk of cancer when following a vegan diet.

Benefit Six: It may lower your blood sugar levels

When you adopt a vegan diet, you may be able to regulate your blood sugar levels more easily. Since vegan diets tend to be lower in sugary, processed foods, they can help to prevent or control type-2 diabetes. For anyone who is diabetic or pre-diabetic, this gives a range of benefits. Not only will it potentially help to control your condition, but it may also lower other risk factors, such as unhealthy weight. Of course, it is always important to consult a medical professional before embarking on a new diet if there are risk factors that affect your health.

Benefit Seven: Your mental health could experience a boost

It is not solely your physical health that could improve when you switch to a vegan diet. Scientific studies have shown that eating vegan, either full-time or part-time, could improve your mental and emotional wellbeing. The fact that vegan diets tend to be higher in fruit and vegetables than meat-based diets can also help your mental health. Fruit and veggies are rich in essential nutrients that can give your mental wellbeing a crucial boost.

Research has shown that specific vitamins and minerals such as iron, calcium, magnesium, folate and omega-3 are all excellent mood-boosting nutrients. These tend to be extremely prevalent in plant-based foods and a vegan diet will facilitate increased intake of these. So, if you are finding that your mood is in a slump or you are experiencing anxiety then a vegan diet could be one way to help alleviate this.

Furthermore, many vegans report that they feel lighter and happier once they change over to a vegan lifestyle. This could be partly because of the foods that they are eating, but also because of the foods that they are *not* eating. Researchers found that people who consume a diet that is heavier in animal products often experience a lower mood than those who follow a vegetarian or vegan diet.

Benefit Eight: Glowing skin and silky hair

Plant-based foods are rich in antioxidants, as well as being full of essential vitamins and minerals. The restriction of animal products, such as dairy foods, is often linked with an improvement in the way your skin and hair look and feel. Vitamin C, vitamin E, vitamin A and zinc are all associated with healthier skin and hair and these nutrients are significantly more abundant in a vegan diet.

Therefore, you could experience significant benefits to your appearance when you adopt a vegan diet. Conditions such as acne have been shown to improve during trials with people who transition from a meat-based diet to a plant-based diet. You may even find that the appearance of some signs of ageing recedes as there has been anecdotal evidence that this can be the case.

Benefit Nine: Reduction in aches and pains

There have been various studies that have demonstrated the benefits of a vegan diet when it comes to reducing inflammation in the body. For example, it has been found that following a vegan diet can reduce C-reactive protein which is linked to both chronic and acute inflammation. Therefore, a plant-based diet can lessen or alleviate the symptoms of conditions such as arthritis.

During trials, many participants reported that a vegan diet caused their aches and pains from osteoarthritis to reduce and they experienced an increase in energy and wellbeing. Therefore, if you are suffering from aches and pains that are related to a condition such as arthritis, changing to a vegan diet could help you. Of course, always consult your doctor before making any extreme changes to your lifestyle.

As a bonus, vegan diets can also be suitable for people with allergies or intolerances to certain foods and may ease discomfort if you have found that you are sensitive to foods such as dairy or eggs.

Benefit Ten: Vegan diets are cruelty-free

Of course, it might seem that eating a cruelty-free diet benefits the health of the animals more than it benefits you. However, if you have been experiencing guilt over eating meat, fish or other animal products, then eliminating them from your diet could also eliminate the guilt. Consequently, you might feel happier and find that your mood is elevated.

Why Veganism is an Eco-friendly option

In the modern world, many of us are concerned about being more eco-friendly, protecting the environment and ensuring that we reduce our carbon footprint.

Veganism, including vegan diets and fully vegan lifestyles, have often been shown to have much more positive environmental impacts. For example, eating a vegan diet can ensure that you protect the oceans, earth and air.

In general, vegan foods are more sustainable than animal products and consequently, this can help to reduce any negative ecological impacts and cut your carbon footprint. What's more, a vegan lifestyle can save a significant amount of water and grains when it comes to farming which also benefits the environment.

Animal agriculture is often associated with increasing carbon emissions and contributing to climate change and global warming. By sticking to plant-based foods that have been grown and harvested sustainably, you can ensure that your vegan diet is extremely beneficial for the environment and does not cause undue harm. Incorporating veganism into your lifestyle can help to play a part in reducing these risk factors to the environment and can ensure that you do your bit to save the planet for future generations.

BREAKFASTS

They say that breakfast is the most important meal of the day and vegan breakfasts should be a satisfying delightful feast that will give you the nutrition and flavour combination to set you up for the rest of your day. These delicious vegan breakfasts are quick and simple to prepare, even when you're in a rush.

TROPICAL PANCAKES

With lashings of banana, pineapple and coconut, these tropical vegan breakfast pancakes provide the perfect breakfast treat for all the family.

Time: 30 minutes | Serves: 4

INGREDIENTS:

- 100 g plain flour
- 1 ½ tbsp caster sugar
- 2 tsp demerara sugar
- 1 tsp baking powder
- 200 ml coconut milk + 50 ml coconut milk
- ½ pineapple, sliced into rings
- 1 banana, sliced
- 1 passion fruit
- 2 tbsp coconut oil

METHOD:

1. Into a large bowl, sift the flour and the baking powder and add in the caster sugar.
2. Whisk the coconut milk into the dry mixture until you have worked out any lumps and have a smooth batter.
3. Add 1 tbsp of coconut oil to a frying pan and heat it over a medium-hot stove. Ladle in some batter to the pan, just using enough batter to thinly coat the bottom of the pan.
4. When the pancake is cooked on the underside flip it and cook the other side until it is browned.
5. Repeat with each pancake until you have cooked all the pancakes.
6. Meanwhile, in another frying pan, heat the other 1 tbsp coconut oil and place the bananas and pineapple rings into the hot oil. Sprinkle the demerara sugar over the top and add in the other 50 ml of coconut milk.
7. Fry the fruit until it has caramelised and then serve it over the top of the cooked pancakes.

PER SERVING:
CALORIES: 200 | CARBS: 25 G | FAT: 10 G | PROTEIN: 3 G

VEGAN LEMON BREAKFAST BREAD

Ideal for a quick breakfast, prepare this in advance and eat it on the go!

Time: 80 minutes | Serves: 6

INGREDIENTS:

- 120 g plain flour
- 1 ½ tsp baking powder
- ¼ tsp bicarbonate of soda
- ½ tsp salt
- 200 g caster sugar

- 125 g dairy-free yoghurt
- 60 ml coconut oil, melted
- 60 ml lemon juice
- Zest of 1 large lemon
- 1 tsp vanilla extract

METHOD:

1. Preheat the oven to 180 degrees Celsius and grease a loaf tin.
2. Add flour, baking powder, bicarbonate of soda, salt and sugar to a large bowl and whisk to combine.
3. To another bowl, add yoghurt, oil, lemon juice, lemon zest and vanilla and whisk.
4. Pour wet batter into the dry mixture and stir until the mixture is smooth and thick.
5. Transfer the batter to the loaf tin and bake for 50-60 minutes until the bread is golden and set.
6. Remove from the oven and allow it to cool before removing it from the tin.
7. Serve in thick slices with jam or vegan margarine.

PER SERVING:
CALORIES: 280 | CARBS: 26 G | FAT: 18 G | PROTEIN: 4 G

RASPBERRY CHIA PUDDING

A healthy and satisfying breakfast, Raspberry Chia Pudding may well become a regular staple on your breakfast menu. Taking only minutes to prep, it is ideal for a quick breakfast fix.

Time: 10 minutes | Serves: 2

INGREDIENTS:

- 4 tbsp chia seeds
- 250 ml almond milk
- 1 tbsp maple syrup
- 1 tsp vanilla extract
- 100 g raspberries

METHOD:

1. In a large bowl mix the chia seeds, almond milk, vanilla and maple syrup.
2. Divide the mixture into two smaller bowls and cover each bowl with a layer of cling wrap.
3. Transfer the bowls to the refrigerator and chill overnight.
4. When you are ready to serve them, top each bowl with the raspberries.

PER SERVING:
CALORIES: 250 | 24 G | FAT: 12 G | PROTEIN: 5 G

FRUITY PORRIDGE

Did you know that oats are one of the healthiest foods for your heart? Bursting with vitamins, minerals and essential fibre, this breakfast dish is the treat your body is craving.

Time: 20 minutes | Serves: 4

INGREDIENTS:

- 100 g porridge oats
- 500 ml oat or almond milk
- 100 g blueberries
- 100 g raspberries

METHOD:

1. To a large saucepan add the oats and milk and simmer for ten minutes, stirring regularly, until the mixture starts to thicken. Add more milk if you prefer a thinner consistency.
2. Meanwhile, add the blueberries and strawberries to a separate saucepan and allow them to soften.
3. Remove both pans from the heat and ladle the porridge into four bowls.
4. Divide the berry mixture between the four bowls, topping each one equally with the cooked fruit and serve.

PER SERVING:
CALORIES: 480 | 38 G | FAT: 12 G | PROTEIN: 9

BREAKFAST SUPER SMOOTHIE

For an easy morning meal, whip up a super smoothie. Designed to provide you with two of your five a day and packed with crucial vitamins, this smoothie might just be the best smoothie you have ever tasted.

Time: 10 minutes | Serves: 4

INGREDIENTS:

- 1 mango, peeled and diced
- 2 kiwi fruit, peeled and diced
- 100 g raspberries
- 100 g strawberries, hulled
- 1 banana, sliced
- 600 ml pineapple juice
- 10 ice cubes

METHOD:

1. Add all the ingredients into a blender and blitz.
2. Serve in glasses.

PER SERVING:
CALORIES: 180 | 40 G | FAT: 2 G | PROTEIN: 3 G

AVOCADO TOAST

Simple and easy, tasty avocados spread on hot, crispy toast is a breakfast delight.

Time: 10 minutes | Serves: 2

INGREDIENTS:

- 4 slices of sourdough bread
- 1 avocado, stone removed
- 1 tbsp maple syrup

METHOD:

1. Toast the bread in a toaster until it is golden brown.
2. Meanwhile, mash the avocado with the maple syrup.
3. Spread the avocado mixture over the toast and serve.

PER SERVING:
CALORIES: 350 | 22 G | FAT: 10 G | PROTEIN: 4 G

MUSHROOM WAFFLES

This is a delicious dish that is perfect for breakfast or brunch and can even be served as a quick and easy lunch option.

Time: 50 minutes | Serves: 4

INGREDIENTS:

- 350 ml rice milk
- 1 tsp lemon juice
- 2 tbsp coconut oil, melted
- 65 g cooked, cooled and mashed sweet potato
- 85 g plain flour
- 1 tbsp baking powder
- 90 g polenta
- 1 tbsp maple syrup
- 1 tsp soy sauce
- 4 portobello mushrooms, sliced
- 1 tbsp olive oil
- Salt and pepper

METHOD:

1. Preheat your waffle maker.
2. In a large bowl, combine the rice milk and lemon juice and then stir in the mashed sweet potato.
3. In a separate bowl, mix the plain flour, polenta and baking powder and then whisk in the wet batter until the mixture is thoroughly combined. Season with salt and pepper.
4. Fill the waffle maker with some of the batter and leave it to cook for 5 minutes. Remove the cooked waffle and repeat until you have made 4 waffles.
5. While the waffles are cooking, in a small bowl mix the maple syrup and soy sauce. Coat the mushrooms in the mixture.
6. In a frying pan, heat the oil over a medium heat. Fry the mushrooms until they have browned.
7. Serve the mushroom mixture over the waffles.

PER SERVING:
CALORIES: 240 | CARBS: 30 G | FAT: 10 G | PROTEIN: 8 G

HOMEMADE GRANOLA

Prepare your granola in advance and eat it at your leisure. Excellent when served with lashings of oat, almond or coconut milk.

Time: 40 minutes | Serves: 20

INGREDIENTS:

- 250 ml coconut oil, melted
- 1 tsp cinnamon
- 250 ml maple syrup
- 1 tsp salt
- 550 g rolled oats
- 300 g blanched, sliced almonds
- 300 g sultanas

METHOD:

1. Preheat the oven to 150 degrees Celsius and line a baking tray.
2. To a large bowl, add the coconut oil, maple syrup, cinnamon and salt and whisk to ensure that all the ingredients are thoroughly combined.
3. Add in the oats and the almonds and stir them through the oil and syrup mixture so that they are fully coated.
4. Transfer the mixture to the prepared baking tray and spread it so that you have an even layer.
5. Place the tray in the centre of your preheated oven and bake it for 20 minutes, checking regularly to ensure that it does not burn. Halfway through cooking, remove the tray and stir the granola before returning to the oven.
6. After 20 minutes, remove the tray from the oven and in the sultanas, ensuring that you press down on the granola with utensils to allow the fruit to stick to the granola.
7. Set the tray aside and allow it cool completely.
8. Once the mixture is cooled, store it in a container that is airtight and you can use the granola with chilled dairy-free milk at your leisure for up to one month.

PER SERVING:
CALORIES: 340 | CARBS: 42 G | FAT: 18 G | PROTEIN: 6 G

TRADITIONAL FULL ENGLISH BREAKFAST

When you need maximum fuel to get you through the day, there is nothing better than this vegan twist on the Traditional English breakfast. Packed full of nutrients, vitamins and healthy fats, it will fill you up and energise you for the day ahead. This is an excellent option for a weekend breakfast treat when you have more time to prepare a leisurely breakfast. For a lighter version, simply halve the quantities.

Time: 50 minutes | Serves: 4

INGREDIENTS:

- 400 g cherry tomatoes
- 60 ml olive oil
- 4 portobello mushrooms
- 2 tsp soy sauce
- ½ tsp paprika
- 1 tbsp maple syrup
- 30 g vegan butter
- 2 Maris Piper potatoes
- 3 tbsp smooth peanut butter

- 700 g silken tofu
- 100 g vegan parmesan cheese
- 2 cloves of garlic, minced
- 1 tsp turmeric
- 8 vegan sausages
- 400 g baked beans
- 2 avocados, halved, stones removed and thinly sliced

METHOD:

1. Place the potatoes into a large saucepan and cover them with water. Place the pan onto the stove and bring the water to a boil for 10 minutes. Remove the pan from the heat and drain the water and set the potatoes aside to cool in a clean bowl.
2. When the potatoes are fully cool, peel them and roughly grate them before combining the grated potatoes with the peanut butter. Cover the bowl and place it into the refrigerator.
3. Preheat the oven to 200 degrees Celsius. Spread the cherry tomatoes evenly over the tray and pour the olive oil over them. Place the tray into the oven and bake for 25-30 minutes.

4. While the tomatoes are baking, pour the soy sauce and maple syrup into a bowl and add in the paprika. Mix them thoroughly to combine and then dip the portobello mushrooms into the mixture and coat them thoroughly.
5. Add the vegan butter to a large frying pan and heat it. Place the mushrooms into the pan and fry them until they turn golden brown but do not allow them to burn.
6. Meanwhile, place the vegan sausages onto a baking tray or grill pan and cook them according to the instructions on the pack.
7. Place the baked beans into a saucepan and start to cook them slowly over a low heat, stirring occasionally as they cook.
8. Remove the mushrooms from the pan and transfer them to a plate. Cover loosely with foil to keep them warm until you are ready to serve them.
9. Return to the frying pan and melt a tsp of vegan butter in the pan. Remove the potato mixture from the fridge and divide it into 8 scoops. Shape them into a hash brown form and fry each one for 4 minutes on each side. Remove the hash browns from the pan and transfer them to a plate lined with kitchen towels to allow them to drain.
10. Add another tsp of vegan butter into the pan and crumble in the silken tofu. Grate in the vegan parmesan cheese, turmeric and minced garlic. Add in a tsp of olive oil and fry for 4-5 minutes until the tofu is fully cooked.
11. To assemble your breakfast, take four plates and place 2 vegan sausages, 1 portobello mushroom and 2 hash browns onto each plate. Divide the other ingredients equally between the four plates and garnish each breakfast with one sliced avocado half. Season to taste with salt and freshly ground black pepper before serving.

PER SERVING:
CALORIES: 650 | CARBS: 60 G | FAT: 28 G | PROTEIN: 44 G

FRENCH TOAST

An eggless French toast that tastes even better than the original version. Sprinkled with a touch of cinnamon and brown sugar, you will not be able to resist this dish in the mornings.

Time: 30 minutes | Serves: 2

INGREDIENTS:

- 1 tbsp finely ground chia seeds
- 190 ml non-dairy milk (such as almost, oat, rice or soya)
- 1 ½ tsp maple syrup
- ½ tsp vanilla extract
- ½ tsp cinnamon powder
- 4 thick slices of seeded wholemeal bread
- 4 tsp coconut oil
- 2 tsp soft brown sugar

METHOD:

1. In a large bowl, place the ground chia seeds, milk, maple syrup, vanilla extract and cinnamon. Mix them thoroughly to combine.
2. Heat 1 tsp of the coconut oil in a large frying pan over a medium heat on the stove.
3. Dip 1 slice of the bread into the batter mixture and fully coat it. Do not allow it to turn soggy but ensure that it is moist.
4. Place the slice of bread onto the frying pan and cook it for 3-4 minutes on each side before transferring it to a place.
5. Repeat the process with the other three slices of bread and sprinkle each one with ½ tsp of brown sugar.
6. You can top the French toast with your favourite toppings such as strawberries, blueberries or whipped vegan cream.

PER SERVING:
CALORIES: 170 | CARBS: 32 G | FAT: 3 G | PROTEIN: 6 G

BREAKFAST MUFFINS

Perfect for freezing or keeping on hand for a quick breakfast or brunch snack, breakfast muffins are exceptionally rich in fibre.

Time: 50 minutes | Serves: 12

INGREDIENTS:

- 50 g soft brown sugar
- 150 g muesli
- 160 g plain white flour
- 1 eating apple
- 2 tbsp coconut oil
- 1 tsp baking powder
- 250 ml almond milk
- 50 g pecan nuts
- 3 tbsp smooth peanut butter
- 4 tbsp demerara sugar

METHOD:

1. Preheat the oven to 180 degrees Celsius and place cake cases inside a 12-hole muffin or cupcake tin.
2. In a large bowl combine two-thirds of the muesli with the brown sugar, baking powder and flour.
3. Peel the apple and grate it into a bowl and add in the milk, coconut oil and 2 tbsp of the peanut butter.
4. Pour the wet ingredients into the dry mixture and thoroughly combine them.
5. Divide the batter equally between the muffin cases and ensure each one is level.
6. In a clean bowl mix together the remaining 50 g of muesli, 1 tbsp of peanut butter, pecans and demerara sugar and divide it equally over the very top of each muffin.
7. Place the muffins into the preheated oven to bake for 30 minutes until they have risen and turned golden brown.
8. Remove them from the oven and place them onto a cooling rack to cool down. You can serve them immediately, store them in an airtight container for up to three days or freeze them for up to one month.

PER SERVING:
CALORIES: 230 | CARBS: 28 G | FAT: 10 G | PROTEIN: 5 G

GRAPEFRUIT SALAD

When you're in the mood for a light and refreshing breakfast or you're seeking a low-calorie option, this dish will satisfy you without making you feel overly full.

Time: 10 minutes | Serves: 2

INGREDIENTS:

- 2 large grapefruits
- 2 blood oranges
- 500 g vegan yoghurt
- 75 g pistachio nuts
- 2 tbsp maple syrup

METHOD:

1. Remove the skin from the grapefruits and the oranges with a sharp knife. Slice them thickly and divide the slices equally into two serving bowls. Drizzle each bowl with 1 tbsp of maple syrup.
2. Divide the vegan yoghurt over the top of the two bowls.
3. Chop the pistachio nuts and sprinkle them over the top to finish before serving.

PER SERVING:
CALORIES: 210 | CARBS: 18 G | FAT: 14 G | PROTEIN: 4 G

GREEN KALE SMOOTHIE

Smoothies are an excellent breakfast option and this green smoothie is jam-packed with an array of vital nutrients such a vitamin C that are crucial to boosting your health and wellbeing. Enjoy one of these smoothies before work or before a workout!

Time: 10 minutes | Serves: 2

INGREDIENTS:

- 50 g kale
- 100 g frozen pineapple chunks
- 1 banana
- ½ avocado, peeled and stone removed
- 1 medium piece of fresh ginger, peeled
- ½ lime, juiced
- 1 tbsp cashews
- 100 ml apple juice

METHOD:

1. Add the kale, pineapple, banana, avocado, ginger, lime juice and cashews to a blender and pour in the apple juice.
2. Blitz until the smoothie is fully blended and pour it into two serving glasses.

PER SERVING:
CALORIES: 160 | CARBS: 7 G | FAT: 10 G | PROTEIN: 5 G

BREAKFAST BANANA BREAD

For a satisfyingly sweet and sumptuous breakfast, this banana bread cannot be beaten. It is a dish that is best prepared the day before as it can be grabbed and taken on the go when your morning is hectic and you're in a rush.

Time: 50 minutes | Serves: 8

INGREDIENTS:

- 225 g plain white flour
- 100 g soft brown sugar
- 3 large overripe bananas
- 80 ml coconut oil, melted
- 1 tbsp baking powder
- 50 g sultanas
- 3 tsp cinnamon

METHOD:

1. Preheat the oven to 190 degrees Celsius and grease and line a large loaf tin.
2. In a large bowl, mash the peeled bananas and add in the melted coconut oil. Pour in the brown sugar and thoroughly combine all the ingredients.
3. Add the plain flour, baking powder and cinnamon and mix it through the batter.
4. Finally, pour in the sultanas and mix them through, ensuring they are evenly distributed.
5. Transfer the mixture to the prepared loaf tin and bake it in the oven for 20 minutes. Remove the tin from the oven, cover it loosely with aluminium foil and return it to the oven for a further 20 minutes.
6. Remove the tin from the oven and allow the banana bread to cool before removing it from the tin. When it is cool, slice it into thick slices and serve.

PER SERVING:
CALORIES: 280 | CARBS: 36 G | FAT: 7 G | PROTEIN: 4 G

STARTERS

These starters are specifically designed to give intense flavour and class to any meal or dinner party. They will satisfy large appetites, and sate your family's hunger. They can also be adapted to make simple lunches.

CAULIFLOWER FRITTERS WITH CREAMY DIP

Crispy battered cauliflower served with a creamy vegan dip is the ultimate taste sensation to start any meal.

Time: 40 minutes | Serves: 4

INGREDIENTS:

For the fritters:
- 1 medium cauliflower, separated into florets
- 500 ml vegetable oil
- 80 g plain flour
- 1 heaped tbsp cornflour
- 120 ml fizzy water
- ½ tsp ground coriander
- Salt and pepper to season

For the dip:
- 100 g plain vegan yoghurt
- 2 handfuls of curly parsley, chopped
- 2 cloves of garlic, minced
- 1 tbsp lemon juice
- 1 tbsp capers
- 2 tbsp olive oil

METHOD:

1. In a large bowl combine the flour, cornflour, fizzy water and coriander. Whisk thoroughly to form a batter.
2. Meanwhile, put the cauliflower in a pan of salted, boiling water and cook for 2-3 minutes then drain and allow it to steam dry.
3. While the cauliflower is drying, add yoghurt, parsley, garlic, lemon juice, capers and olive oil to a bowl and mix them together, then set aside.
4. Pour vegetable oil into a large saucepan and heat it until it is sizzling hot.
5. Coat each floret of cauliflower in the batter and then drop it into the pan, taking care to avoid any splashes of oil. Fry the cauliflower until it turns golden brown and then remove it from the pan and transfer to plates lined with kitchen towels.
6. Allow the oil to drain from the fritters, season with salt and pepper and then serve with the sauce on the side.

PER SERVING:
CALORIES: 410 | CARBS: 4 G | FAT: 30 G | PROTEIN: 8 G

GARLIC MUSHROOM PARCELS

Delicious moreish mushrooms wrapped in a layer of vegan pastry and baked in the oven, this dish will be a winner with dinner party guests and kids alike.

Time: 40 minutes | Serves: 8

INGREDIENTS:

- 1 block or 500 g vegan puff pastry
- 400 g button mushrooms, halved
- 1 large white onion, diced
- 4 cloves of garlic, minced
- 1 tbsp dried mixed herbs
- 1 tbsp olive oil

METHOD:

1. Preheat the oven to 180 degrees Celsius and grease and line a baking tray.
2. In a frying pan, heat the olive oil and then add in the onion, softening it until it turns translucent.
3. Add the minced garlic to the pan, cooking for a further 1-2 minutes.
4. Add in the mushrooms and mixed herbs and cook for another 5 minutes.
5. Meanwhile, roll out the puff pastry and divide it into 8 equal squares. Brush each square with a little olive oil.
6. Once the mushroom mixture is fully cooked, remove it from the heat and allow it to cool down for a few minutes.
7. When the mixture is cool, spoon an equal amount onto each of the puff pastry squares and then fold the corners of each square to make 8 little parcels.
8. Transfer the parcels to a baking tray and bake for 15-20 minutes until they have turned golden brown and puffed up.

PER SERVING:
CALORIES: 220 | CARBS: 22 G | FAT: 12 G | PROTEIN: 4 G

BUTTERNUT SQUASH SOUP

With its rich, deep flavours and pleasing textures, butternut squash makes the perfect soup base.

Time: 50 minutes | Serves: 4

INGREDIENTS:

- 1 large butternut squash, peeled, seeds removed and diced
- 1 large white onion, diced
- 2 cloves of garlic, minced
- 15 ml olive oil
- 40 ml dry sherry

- 500 ml water with 1 vegan-friendly vegetable stock cube dissolved into it
- 1 tsp dried sage
- 1 handful of fresh parsley, chopped
- Salt and ground black pepper to season

METHOD:

1. Heat the olive oil in a large pan or stockpot over a medium heat on the stove and add in the onions when the oil is sizzling. Fry for around 5 minutes until the onion softens and becomes translucent.
2. Add in the diced squash and the garlic and fry for a further 5 minutes.
3. Pour in the vegetable stock and the sherry and add in the dried sage.
4. Cover the pan and leave it to simmer for 20-25 minutes until the butternut squash is soft and tender.
5. Transfer the soup to a blender or use a soup blending extension to liquidise the mixture. You can blend it more for a smoother texture or leave it chunkier if you prefer. Serve piping hot, season with salt and pepper to taste and garnish with parsley.

PER SERVING:
CALORIES: 220 | CARBS: 24 G | FAT: 7 G | PROTEIN: 5 G

ZESTY RICE AND BEAN SALAD

This quick and simple cold salad is an excellent starter and can also be packed up in a lunchbox for work or school.

Time: 30 minutes | Serves: 2

INGREDIENTS:

- 150 g white rice
- 300 ml water
- 400 g tinned kidney beans
- ½ cucumber, diced
- 100 g cherry tomatoes, halved

- 50 ml olive oil
- 1 tbsp lemon juice
- ½ tsp black pepper
- ½ chilli powder

METHOD:

1. Pour the water into a large saucepan and add the rice. Bring it to a boil and then put a lid on the pan and reduce the heat to simmer for 15 minutes.
2. Meanwhile, drain and rinse the kidney beans and place them in a bowl. Add in the cucumber and tomatoes.
3. In a separate bowl, combine the olive oil, lemon juice, black pepper and chilli powder, whisking them to ensure they are thoroughly mixed.
4. Pour the dressing over the kidney beans mixture and toss it through.
5. Remove the rice from the heat and allow it to cool completely.
6. When you are ready to serve, combine the cold rice and kidney beans mixture and stir them together.

PER SERVING:
CALORIES: 320 | CARBS: 22 G | FAT: 16 G | PROTEIN: 14 G

ITALIAN BRUSCHETTA

Bruschetta is a staple of the Italian diet. With its rich tomato and garlicky flavours, it is a light option that will pique the appetite in preparation for the main course.

Time: 10 minutes | Serves: 4

INGREDIENTS:

- 1 baguette, sliced into 10-12 slices around 2 cm thick
- 3 beefsteak tomatoes, diced
- 15 ml olive oil
- 3 tbsp fresh basil, finely chopped
- ½ tsp salt
- ¼ tsp ground black pepper

METHOD:

1. To a bowl add the diced tomatoes, basil, olive oil, salt and black pepper.
2. Cover the bowl with cling wrap and set it aside on the worktop to allow the flavours of oil and basil to infuse into the tomatoes.
3. Toast your slices of baguette to a golden brown, ensuring that the bread does not burn. You can either use a toaster or lay the baguette slices onto a grill pan and grill them for 3-4 minutes, turning during cooking.
4. Using a slotted spoon to remove any excess moisture, transfer your tomato mixture onto the toasted bread, season with a little extra black pepper and serve.

PER SERVING:
CALORIES: 180 | CARBS: 12 G | FAT: 4 G | PROTEIN: 2 G

STUFFED BAKED BEEFSTEAK TOMATOES

These juicy tomatoes, stuffed with couscous, are an ideal light starter that will set the perfect tone for any dinner party or family meal. Loved equally by vegans and non-vegans alike, they can also double as a side or as a light lunch.

Time: 30 minutes | Serves: 4

INGREDIENTS:

- 4 beefsteak tomatoes
- 60 ml olive oil
- 2 cloves of garlic, minced
- 100 g couscous
- 1 handful fresh flat-leaf parsley, finely chopped
- Salt and black pepper to season.

METHOD:

1. Preheat the oven to 180 degrees Celsius and grease and line a baking tray.
2. Prepare the couscous according to the pack instructions.
3. Slice the tops off the tomatoes and set them aside. Scoop out the flesh and place it into a large bowl.
4. Combine the tomato flesh with the minced garlic, olive oil, parsley and couscous and season with salt and pepper to taste.
5. Place the tomatoes on the prepared baking tray and fill them with the couscous mixture, ensuring you divide it equally. Place the tops back onto the tomatoes and place the tray into the oven for 25 minutes to bake.
6. Remove the tray from the oven and serve hot.

PER SERVING:
CALORIES: 190 | CARBS: 18 G | FAT: 11 G | PROTEIN: 4 G

ITALIAN PANZANELLA

Originating in Tuscany, this traditional Italian bread-based salad is a superlative summer starter. Light and refreshing, yet equally delicious and satisfying, you can also serve it in larger portions as a healthy vegan main course.

Time: 40 minutes | Serves: 4

INGREDIENTS:

- 1 ciabatta loaf, stale
- 1 medium red onion, finely diced
- 600 g heritage tomatoes, diced
- 3 tbsp capers, rinsed and dried
- 300 g jar of red peppers, drained, rinsed and chopped
- 2 tbsp red wine vinegar
- 1 bunch of fresh basil, roughly chopped
- 90 ml olive oil
- ¼ tsp sea salt
- ¼ tsp ground black pepper

METHOD:

1. Cut the ciabatta into small pieces and place it onto a plate. Allow it to sit in a warm place for 30-40 minutes to fully dry out.
2. In a large bowl, place the diced tomatoes and season them with the sea salt and black pepper.
3. Add the capers, peppers, onion and ciabatta to the bowl. Using your hands, toss the salad thoroughly.
4. In a separate bowl, combine the vinegar and olive oil and drizzle the liquid over the salad before tossing it through.
5. Toss the basil leaves into the salad and combine.

PER SERVING:
CALORIES: 360 | CARBS: 38 G | FAT: 21 G | PROTEIN: 9 G

CREAM OF TOMATO SOUP

Is there anything more comforting on a cold winter's evening than a bowl of heart-warming tomato soup? Made with vegan cream, this rich and delectable starter is always a universal crowd-pleaser for adults and children.

Time: 35 minutes | Serves: 4

INGREDIENTS:

- 800 g tinned whole tomatoes
- 1 large white onion, finely diced
- 1 clove of garlic, minced
- 1 tbsp olive oil
- 1 tbsp vegan margarine
- 700 ml vegan vegetable stock, prepared with 3 vegan stock cubes
- 35 g plain flour
- 1 ½ tsp sugar
- 180 ml almond milk
- ¼ tsp sea salt
- ¼ tsp freshly ground black pepper
- 1 handful fresh flat-leaf parsley, finely chopped
- 50 ml vegan sour cream

METHOD:

1. Place the oil and the vegan margarine into a large saucepan or stockpot and heat on the stove over a medium heat until the margarine is melted and sizzling.
2. Add in the onion and cook for around five minutes until it turns soft and translucent. Then add in the garlic and cook for another 1-2 minutes.
3. Next, sift in the flour and stir it into the onion and garlic mixture, coating them with the flour. Allow the mixture to cook for a further minute.
4. Pour in the prepared stock, tinned tomatoes (including any juice in the can), salt, pepper and sugar.
5. Stir constantly as you simmer it over a medium-high heat and keep an eye out to ensure that the flour does not stick to the bottom or sides of the pan.
6. Turn down the heat to a low heat and cover the pan. Allow the soup to simmer for 20-25 minutes.
7. Remove the pan from the heat and allow it to cool down. Once it is cool, transfer it to a blender and pulse until the texture is smooth and silky.
8. Pour the soup back into the pan, reheat it and add in the almond milk.
9. When the soup is piping hot, divide it equally between four bowls and stir the sour cream into each bowl. Garnish with parsley to serve.

PER SERVING:
CALORIES: 240 | CARBS: 11 G | FAT: 9 G | PROTEIN: 4 G

SUMMER OLIVE SALAD

Quick and simple to put together, no cooking is involved in this salad. It is an excellent and light choice to start any meal and is extremely healthy.

Time: 15 minutes | Serves: 4

INGREDIENTS:

- 2 little gem lettuces, shredded
- 1 cucumber, diced
- 200 g cherry tomatoes, halved
- 100 g black olives, pitted
- 100 g green olives, pitted
- 1 green bell pepper, stalk removed, de-seeded, and finely chopped
- 60 ml olive oil
- 20 ml balsamic vinegar
- 1 handful of basil leaves, finely chopped

METHOD:

1. In a large salad bowl, toss together the lettuce, cucumber, tomatoes, olives and bell pepper.
2. In a separate bowl, pour in the olive oil and vinegar and pour it over the salad, tossing well.
3. Sprinkle the salad with the basil and mix it through so it is evenly distributed before serving.

PER SERVING:
CALORIES: 100 | CARBS: 7 G | FAT: 2 G | PROTEIN: 1 G

CREAMY ASPARAGUS SOUP

The humble asparagus makes for an incredible soup. Enhanced with fresh herbs and a touch of freshly ground black pepper, this soup will be adored by anyone who samples it.

Time: 55 minutes | Serves: 4

INGREDIENTS:

- 1 ½ tbsp olive oil
- 1 medium white onion, diced
- 2 small cloves of garlic, minced
- 600 g asparagus, ends removed and chopped
- 2 small Maris Piper potatoes, peeled and cubed
- 650 ml vegetable broth, prepared with 2 vegan-friendly stock cubes
- 220 ml unsweetened almond milk
- Juice of 1 lemon
- 1 small handful of chives, finely chopped
- Sea salt and ground black pepper to season

METHOD:

1. Preheat the oven to 200 degrees Celsius and grease a baking tray. Spread the asparagus over the tray and drizzle it with 1 tbsp of olive oil. Season the asparagus with salt and pepper, ensuring the oil, salt and pepper are evenly distributed over all the spears.
2. Place the asparagus into the oven for 10-15 minutes until the asparagus starts to soften.
3. Meanwhile, pour the rest of the olive oil into a large saucepan or stockpot and heat it on the stove over a medium heat. Place the onion and the garlic into the pan and heat them until the onions are starting to soften.
4. Season the mixture with salt and pepper, add in the potatoes and continue to cook the veggies for a further 5-10 minutes.
5. Pour the prepared vegetable stock into the pan and then add in the almond milk. Bring the liquid to a boil and then lower the heat until it is simmering. Allow the mixture to simmer for around 20 minutes.
6. Add in the roasted asparagus and cook for 5 minutes. Then, remove the soup from the heat and allow it to cool slightly before transferring it to a blender.
7. Pulse the mixture until the texture turns smooth and the soup looks creamy. You may need to blend the soup in batches if your blender is not large enough or you can leave the soup in the pan and use a soup blender.
8. Return the soup to the pan and heat it through, then remove from the heat and pour in the lemon juice and add the chives, stirring them through the soup thoroughly before serving.

PER SERVING:
CALORIES: 152 | CARBS: 18 G | FAT: 5 G | PROTEIN: 7 G

COURGETTE KEBAB SKEWERS

These steaming hot skewers of courgettes paired with other seasonal vegetables can be tailored to your preferences. Courgettes are undoubtedly the star of this dish, but you can select the supporting acts!

Time: 30 minutes | Serves: 4

INGREDIENTS:

- 2 large courgettes, peeled and cubed
- 200 g button mushrooms, halved
- 200 g cherry tomatoes, halved
- 1 red bell pepper, de-seeded, stalk removed and diced
- 40 ml olive oil
- 20 ml cider vinegar
- 2 cloves of garlic, minced

METHOD:

1. Preheat the oven to 180 degrees Celsius and grease a baking tray.
2. Take your skewers and place each vegetable alternately onto them. You can use other seasonal vegetables in place of the ones in the recipe if you choose.
3. In a small bowl, mix the olive oil, vinegar and minced garlic.
4. Place the vegetable skewers onto the baking tray and drizzle some of the olive oil mixture over them. Put the tray into the oven to bake for 20-25 minutes, keeping a close eye on them to ensure the veggies do not burn.
5. Remove the tray from the oven and drizzle the remaining olive oil mixture over the skewers before serving.

PER SERVING:
CALORIES: 160 | CARBS: 12 G | FAT: 7 G | PROTEIN: 4 G

RADDISH AND BUTTERBEAN SALAD

A unique and innovative salad that will tantalise the tastebuds and revolutionise your views on the traditional salad.

Time: 15 minutes | Serves: 4

INGREDIENTS:

- 800 g tinned butterbeans, drained, rinsed and dried
- 200 g radishes, ends trimmed and sliced thinly
- 400 g cherry tomatoes
- 2 cloves of garlic, minced
- ½ cucumber, seeds removed and thinly sliced
- ½ lemon, juiced
- 1 small bunch of parsley, finely chopped
- 1 small bunch of mint, finely chopped
- 1 tbsp olive oil
- Salt and black pepper to season

METHOD:

1. Combine the parsley, mint, garlic, olive oil and lemon juice in a small bowl. Season to taste with the salt and pepper.
2. Place the butterbeans, cucumber, tomatoes and radishes into a separate bowl and pour the dressing mixture over the top. Toss the salad thoroughly and serve.

PER SERVING:
CALORIES: 220 | CARBS: 25 G | FAT: 6 G | PROTEIN: 12 G

INDIAN DHAL

This traditional dhal is full of rich and aromatic Asian spices. It will take you on a journey of discovery. As a bonus, it is extremely healthy and will impress everyone, including any non-vegans in your circle of family and friends.

Time: 45 minutes | Serves: 4

INGREDIENTS:

- 1 large red onion, finely diced
- 1 medium red chilli, thinly sliced
- 1 clove of garlic, minced
- 1 medium piece of fresh ginger, peeled and roughly chopped
- 2 large sweet potatoes, peeled and evenly diced
- 600 ml vegetable stock prepared with 2 vegan-friendly stock cubes
- 80 g spinach
- 250 g red lentils, rinsed
- 2 tsp cumin powder
- 2 tsp ground turmeric
- 1 tbsp sesame oil
- Salt and pepper to season

METHOD:

1. Pour the sesame oil into a large pan and heat it over a medium heat on the stove. Then, reduce the heat to low and add the red onion to the pan. Cook for 10 minutes until the onion softens.
2. Add the garlic to the ginger, chilli, turmeric and cumin to the pan and cook for a further 2 minutes.
3. Add the sweet potato cubes and stir to ensure the mixture is thoroughly combined.
4. Pour in the vegetable stock and lentils and season with salt and pepper.
5. Bring the mixture to a boil and turn down the heat to a simmer. Cover the pan and leave it to cook for 20-25 minutes.
6. Remove the lid from the pan and add the spinach. Allow it to wilt in the mixture before removing the pan from the heat and serve piping hot.

PER SERVING:
CALORIES: 410 | CARBS: 66 G | FAT: 6 G | PROTEIN: 20 G

VEGAN QUESADILLAS

Simple to prepare and full of flavour, these are quesadillas with a twist. The traditional Mexican dish is prepared with vegan cheese and deliver an excellent depth of flavour.

Time: 25 minutes | Serves: 4

INGREDIENTS:

- 4 tortilla wraps, warmed
- 1 large sweet potato, peeled and grated
- 80 g spinach leaves
- 200 g tinned black beans, drained, rinsed and dried
- 200 g tinned sweetcorn, drained, rinsed and dried
- 3 tbsp olive oil
- ½ tsp ground cumin
- ½ tsp chilli powder
- 1 tsp smoked paprika
- 1 handful fresh flat-leaf parsley, finely chopped
- 100 g vegan cheese, grated
- Salt and ground black pepper to season

METHOD:

1. Heat 2 tbsp of olive oil in a frying pan on the stove over a medium heat. When the oil is sizzling, place the grated sweet potato into the pan and fry for 40 seconds.
2. Add in the cumin, paprika and chilli powder and turn down the heat. Leave the mixture to cook for 5-6 minutes, stirring once a minute.
3. Place the spinach leaves into the pan and stir them to combine them with the ingredients. Allow the dish to cook for another 2 minutes.
4. Pour in the corn, beans and chopped parsley and cook for a further 2 minutes. Remove the pan from the heat and season the dish with salt and pepper to taste.
5. In a separate pan, place 1 tbsp of olive oil and heat it. Take one tortilla wrap and place ¼ of the filling on one half of the wrap. Cover the filling with ¼ of the grated cheese and fold the wrap in half. Place the folded tortilla into the pan and cook for 2-3 minutes on each side. Repeat with the other 3 wraps.
6. Transfer each wrap to a plate when it is cooked and use a sharp knife to cut the quesadillas into slices before serving. They are excellent served with salsa, guacamole or vegan sour cream.

PER SERVING:
CALORIES: 320 | CARBS: 33 G | FAT: 19 G | PROTEIN: 12 G

GAZPACHO

Gazpacho is a cold Spanish soup that makes a fantastic starter on a hot summer's day. You can prepare it to a smooth consistency or make it chunkier depending on your personal preferences.

Time: 55 minutes | Serves: 6

INGREDIENTS:

- 8 large ripe tomatoes, roughly chopped
- 1 red or green bell pepper, stalk and seeds removed and diced
- 2 cucumbers, diced
- 4 cloves of garlic, minced
- 2 large sticks of celery, finely chopped
- 1 red onion, diced
- 2 tbsp lemon juice
- 3 tbsp balsamic vinegar
- 3 tbsp red wine vinegar
- 1 tsp salt
- 1 tsp freshly ground black pepper
- 2 tsp fresh basil, finely chopped
- 2 tsp fresh parsley, finely chopped
- 40 ml olive oil

METHOD:

1. In a blender, place the tomatoes, cucumber, red or green pepper, garlic, onion, celery, basil, parsley and lemon juice. Add in the balsamic vinegar and the red wine vinegar and season the mixture with salt and black pepper.
2. Cover with the top of the blender. Pulse until the mixture is smooth.
3. Transfer the soup to a bowl and cover with cling wrap. Place the bowl into the fridge and chill it for 30-40 minutes.
4. When you are ready to serve, remove the soup from the fridge and divide it evenly between four bowls. Drizzle each bowl with 2 tsp of olive oil.

PER SERVING:
CALORIES: 125 | CARBS: 23 G | FAT: 1 G | PROTEIN: 6 G

VEGAN VOL-AU-VENTS

If you're looking to serve finger food at a dinner party, vol-au-vents deliver everything you could ask for in a starter. These vol-au-vents are filled with creamed mushrooms and completely vegan.

Time: 40 minutes | Serves: 4

INGREDIENTS:

- 8 vegan vol-au-vent cases
- 400 g chestnut mushrooms, cleaned and thinly sliced
- 4 cloves of garlic, minced
- 1 tbsp rosemary leaves, chopped and with stems removed
- 1 tbsp plain flour
- 250 ml dairy-free vegan cream
- 1 tbsp olive oil
- ¼ tsp sea salt
- ¼ tsp black pepper
- 1 tsp parsley, finely chopped

METHOD:

1. Heat the olive oil in a large saucepan on the stove over a medium heat. Add the garlic and rosemary to the pan and cook them for 2 minutes.
2. Place the mushrooms in the pan and cook them for 10-15 minutes until they soften and start to brown slightly. Then, add in the flour and stir it through the mixture.
3. Pour in the vegan cream very gradually and stir constantly as you pour. Sprinkle the salt and pepper into the dish and stir thoroughly to combine. Leave the mixture to simmer for 10 minutes.
4. Meanwhile, place the vol-au-vents into a preheated oven and cook them according to the instructions on the pack.
5. Remove the mushrooms from the stove when the vol-au-vents are ready and fill each pastry case to the top with the creamy mushroom mixture. Sprinkle with the chopped parsley to garnish before serving.

PER SERVING:
CALORIES: 220 | CARBS: 17 G | FAT: 15 G | PROTEIN: 6 G

MELON BOATS

Is there anything as deliciously retro as the classic 1970s melon boat? These little starters are a sweet way to begin your meal and have the advantage of cleansing your palate to prepare you for your main course.

Time: 10 minutes | Serves: 4

INGREDIENTS:

- 1 cantaloupe melon
- 8 glace cherries
- 1 lime
- 400 g lemon or lime sorbet

METHOD:

1. Cut the melon into halves, spoon out the seeds and discard them.
2. Slice each melon half into two so that you have four-quarters.
3. Turn each quarter onto its side and cut away the rind at the bottom so that the melon can sit flat and upright without rocking.
4. Using a sharp knife, make slits through the melon flesh but be careful not to cut through the ring at the bottom when you do this.
5. Juice the lime and squeeze the juice over the melon, allowing it to flow into the slits.
6. Place the sorbet on the top of each quarter, dividing it equally.
7. Top with the glace cherries and serve.

PER SERVING:
CALORIES: 120 | CARBS: 8 G | FAT: 3 G | PROTEIN: 2 G

MAIN COURSES

Whether you are serving dinner to your family or hosting the perfect party, these main courses have that "wow factor." You will impress everyone with these swift and simple dishes that have oodles of flavour packed into them.

CREAMY MUSHROOM RISOTTO

This vegan version of the traditional Italian dish is an absolute delight. Its creamy texture and delicious taste will have everyone requesting a second helping.

Time: 50 minutes | Serves: 4

INGREDIENTS:

- 400 g chestnut mushrooms, cleaned and thickly sliced
- 250 g risotto rice
- 3 cloves of garlic, minced
- 120 ml vegan-friendly white wine
- 2 small shallots, finely diced
- 1.2 L vegan vegetable stock
- 60 ml olive oil
- 1 handful of parsley, finely chopped
- ¼ bunch of chives, finely chopped

METHOD:

1. In a large frying pan, heat a little olive oil until it is sizzling and fry the shallots until they soften. Then add in the minced garlic and mushrooms and fry for a further 4-5 minutes. Take 2 tbsp of the prepared vegetable stock and pour it into the pan, stirring it through.

2. Next add in the rice, olive oil and white wine, stirring everything thoroughly.

3. Gradually ladle in the stock, waiting until all the moisture has been absorbed before adding in another ladleful. Cook the risotto for at least 25 minutes, until you have ladled in all the stock.

4. Remove the pan from the heat and add another 2 tsp of olive oil and the herbs before serving.

PER SERVING:
CALORIES: 420 | CARBS: 45 G | FAT: 21 G | PROTEIN: 9 G

POLPETTE AL SUGO

Polpette al Sugo is meatballs in a rich sauce. Of course, this is a vegan version but it does not skimp on taste or texture. A dinner party and family favourite, this is also the perfect dish for a romantic meal at home. Served in a vegan Bolognese sauce, you can feed this to vegans, vegetarians and meat-eaters alike.

Time: 60 minutes | Serves: 4

INGREDIENTS:

For the meatballs:
- 250 g cauliflower, divided into florets, cooked and cooled
- 400 g tinned black beans, drained, rinsed and dried
- 220 g spinach, steamed and squeezed dry to remove all moisture
- 2 cloves of garlic, minced
- 1 tsp of dried mixed herbs
- 150 g rolled oats, ground into a powder
- Salt and black pepper to season

For the Bolognese sauce:
- 800 g tinned chopped tomatoes
- 2 tbsp tomato puree
- 1 handful of fresh basil
- 1 tsp dried oregano
- 2 cloves of garlic, minced
- 1 small white onion, diced
- 200 g mushrooms, diced
- 50 ml olive oil

To serve:
- 250 g spaghetti
- Salt and black pepper to season

METHOD:

1. Grate or finely chop the cooked and dried cauliflower into a large bowl and add in the beans, spinach, garlic and mixed herbs. Mix it all together to thoroughly combine and add in the rolled oats, stirring them through.

2. Using your hands, take small scoops of the mixture and roll them into small balls. Then place on a plate, cover loosely with cling film and chill in the fridge for 1 hour.

3. Preheat the oven to 180 degrees Celsius and remove the balls from the fridge.

4. Add all the sauce ingredients into a blender and blitz until they are roughly blended.

5. Meanwhile, heat a tbsp of olive oil in a frying pan and fry the "meat" balls until they are browned. Line a plate with some kitchen towels and place the balls on the towels to drain.

6. Place the sauce in a large, ovenproof dish and add in the meatballs. Add in the dried spaghetti. Cover the dish with a lid and place it in the oven to cook for 35 minutes.

7. Remove the dish from the oven and serve piping hot. You can grate some vegan parmesan cheese onto the top if you like and season it with salt and black pepper to taste.

PER SERVING:
CALORIES: 410 | CARBS: 38 G | FAT: 22 G | PROTEIN: 4 G

VEGETABLE AND CHICKPEA JALFREZI

When you're in the mood for Indian food, this healthy meal is a lovely option. It's packed full of spices to give you an authentic Indian taste experience.

Time: 40 minutes | Serves: 4

INGREDIENTS:

- ½ butternut squash, peeled, seeds removed and diced
- 2 red onions, diced
- 1 small cauliflower, divided into small florets
- 500 ml passata
- 500 ml cool water
- 15 ml olive oil
- 1 vegan vegetable stock cube
- 1 bunch of coriander, finely chopped
- 400 g tinned chickpeas, drained, rinsed and dried
- 1 yellow pepper, stalk removed, de-seeded and chopped
- 1 red pepper, stalk removed, de-seeded and chopped
- 100 ml vegan cream
- 200 g shop-bought vegan jalfrezi curry paste
- 300 g basmati rice, cooked

METHOD:

1. In a frying pan, cook the onions over a medium heat until they soften.
2. Add in the curry paste and mix it together with the onions and then add in the cauliflower, butternut squash, stock cube, coriander and passata. Mix thoroughly to combine and add in the cool water. Leave the mixture to simmer for 20-25 minutes, adding in extra water if the mixture becomes overly thickened.
3. After 20 minutes, add in the diced peppers and the chickpeas and then cook for a further 20 minutes.
4. Remove from the heat and serve with the cooked rice.

PER SERVING:
CALORIES: 420 | CARBS: 44 G | FAT: 11 G | PROTEIN: 14 G

GRILLED QUNIOA COURGETTES AND TOFU

An excellent source of protein, this delightfully flavoursome South American grain is paired with grilled courgettes to produce a healthy light main course.

Time: 25 minutes | Serves: 4

INGREDIENTS:

- 180 g quinoa, uncooked
- 1 block of firm tofu, sliced
- 450 ml water
- ¼ tsp salt
- 2 large courgettes, sliced
- 4 cloves of garlic, minced
- 100 ml olive oil
- 2 tbsp lemon juice
- 1 handful of mint, finely chopped
- ¼ tsp black pepper

METHOD:

1. Rinse the quinoa in a sieve or colander for 1 minute before fully draining to ensure that any bitterness is removed.
2. Add the water and salt to a large saucepan and bring to a boil and then add in the quinoa.
3. Allow the quinoa to boil for 30 seconds and then turn the heat down and simmer it for 15-20 minutes, checking on it regularly.
4. Meanwhile, in a small bowl, combine the olive oil, lemon juice, minced garlic and mint. Season with black pepper and stir thoroughly. Place the tofu into the bowl and allow it to marinate for 20 minutes.
5. Preheat your grill to a high heat and prepare a grill pan, layering your slices of courgette onto the tray. Remove the tofu from the marinade and place it onto the grill pan. Brush each slice of courgette with a little olive oil and place under the grill for 10 minutes, turning halfway through cooking. After ten minutes remove them from under the grill and immediately place them in the oil mixture while they are still piping hot.
6. Returning to your quinoa, after 15-20 minutes, it should have become fluffy and absorbed the water. Remove it from the pan and transfer it to your serving plates.
7. Add the courgettes and tofu onto the top of it, pouring any extra dressing that is left over the top and season to taste before serving.

PER SERVING:
CALORIES: 450 | CARBS: 22 G | FAT: 32 G | PROTEIN: 18 G

COTTAGE PIE

Topped with a layer of creamy mashed potato, this vegan cottage pie is a heart-warming meal that might just become one of your winter favourites. A one-pot recipe, this dish could not be easier to prepare and cook. It's excellent for when you are short on time and want to make a quick and easy dinner for the kids.

Time: 90 minutes | Serves: 4

INGREDIENTS:

- 300 g Maris Piper potatoes, washed, peeled and diced
- 300 g sweet potatoes, washed, peeled and diced
- 20 g vegan margarine
- 2 cloves of garlic
- 1 large white onion, sliced
- 1 carrot, sliced
- 1 celery stick, thinly sliced
- 1 tbsp ground coriander
- 50 ml olive oil
- 1 tbsp fresh thyme, chopped
- 1 tsp dried rosemary
- 200 g button mushrooms, halved
- 50 ml vegan-friendly red wine
- 50 ml vegan vegetable stock
- 400 g of cooked red lentils
- 1 tbsp lemon juice

METHOD:

1. Preheat the oven to 200 degrees Celsius and grease a large ovenproof dish.
2. Fill a large saucepan with water and cook the chunks of potato and sweet potato by bringing it to a boil and then reducing the heat to simmer for 15 minutes. Drain them and allow them to steam-dry. When they are dry, add in the vegan margarine and mash the potatoes.
3. Heat some olive oil in a large frying pan and add in the onion, carrot, celery, coriander, thyme and rosemary and fry for 5 minutes. Add in the mushrooms and fry for a further 5 minutes until the veggies have softened.
4. Transfer the onion mixture to an oiled stockpot and add in the red wine and the vegetable stock. Add in the lentils. Turn the heat up to medium-high and allow it to cook for 15 minutes.
5. When the liquid has reduced, transfer the whole mixture to the ovenproof dish and cover it with the mash.
6. Place the dish into the oven and cook for 15 minutes. Remove from the oven and finish off under the grill for 10 minutes to brown the potato before serving.

PER SERVING:
CALORIES: 360 | CARBS: 45 G | FAT: 16 G | PROTEIN: 9 G

VEGAN PUFF PASTRY TART

A vegan version of delicious comfort food! Fill it with your preferred veggies and it's a delight to eat.

Time: 40 minutes | Serves: 4

INGREDIENTS:

- 500 g vegan puff pastry
- 1 small head of cauliflower
- 1 small head of broccoli
- 1 large carrot, sliced
- 1 tin of black beans, drained, rinsed and dried
- 1 can of chopped tomatoes, liquid drained
- 1 tbsp dried mixed herbs
- Salt and pepper to season

METHOD:

1. Preheat the oven to 180 degrees Celsius and grease a large baking dish.
2. Divide the puff pastry block into two and roll out both pieces on a floured surface.
3. In a large saucepan, place the vegetables and submerge them in boiling water. Bring to the boil and simmer for 10 minutes before draining. Allow the veg to steam dry for several minutes. Leaving the veggies in the pan, add in the chopped tomatoes, ensuring that you have drained the liquid from the can. Then add in the black beans, the herbs and the salt and pepper and simmer for 5 minutes.
4. Place one sheet of the puff pastry into the baking dish, allowing a little to hang over the sides of the dish. Transfer your veggie filling into the dish on top of the pastry and then place the other sheet of puff pastry over the top. Poke a few holes in the top to allow air to escape.
5. Bake for 20-25 minutes until the pastry has turned golden brown and risen. Serve piping hot.

PER SERVING:
CALORIES: 340 | CARBS: 22 G | FAT: 12 G | PROTEIN: 6 G

FALAFEL BURGERS

These delicious treats are inspired by Middle-Eastern flavours. Made with chickpeas they are full of nutrients and taste great on their own or served on a bun.

Time: 40 minutes | Serves: 4

INGREDIENTS:

- 400 g can of chickpeas, drained, rinsed and dried
- 2 cloves of garlic, minced
- 10 g plain flour
- 1 large red onion, finely diced
- 1 tsp dried coriander
- 1 tsp black pepper
- 2 tsp dried parsley

- 1 tsp cumin powder
- 1 tsp chilli powder
- ½ tsp salt
- 30 ml olive oil
- 8 cherry tomatoes, halved
- 8 slices of cucumber
- 4 lettuce leaves
- 4 burger buns, toasted

METHOD:

1. Preheat the oven to 180 degrees Celsius and grease and line a baking tray.
2. Rinse and fully dry the chickpeas then place them into a blender along with the onion, garlic, parsley, cumin, coriander, chilli powder, salt, oil and plain flour.
3. Blend the mixture until it is smooth but still retains some texture. Remove it from the blender and transfer it to a bowl.
4. Using your hands, scoop a handful of the mixture, roll it into a ball and then flatten to make the shape of a burger patty and repeat until you have four patties.
5. Place the burger patties onto the baking tray and bake for 25 minutes, before removing them from the oven. Serve on the toasted buns and garnish with the lettuce, cucumber and tomato and add your favourite vegan sauce.

PER SERVING:
CALORIES: 370 | CARBS: 28 G | FAT: 14 G | PROTEIN: 14 G

SPICY MEXICAN FAJITAS

Made with strips of tofu and a selection of seasonable vegetables, these fajitas are great served with salsa and guacamole on the side.

Time: 20 minutes | Serves: 4

INGREDIENTS:

- 1 red onion, sliced into rings
- 1 red pepper with the stalk and seeds removed, sliced into strips
- 1 clove of garlic, minced
- 1 tbsp olive oil
- 1 tsp paprika
- 1 tbsp lime juice
- ½ tsp chilli powder
- 1 tsp dried coriander
- ½ tsp cumin powder
- 400 g tinned kidney beans, drained, rinsed and dried
- 4 tortilla wraps, to serve

METHOD:

1. In a large frying pan, heat the olive oil until it is sizzling hot. Add in the onions and soften for 5 minutes. Then, add in the pepper and cook for a further 5 minutes.

2. Add the garlic, paprika, chilli powder, cumin and coriander to the pan and stir well. Then add in the lime juice. Finally, add in the kidney beans and cook them through until the mixture is piping hot.

3. Wrap the tortillas in aluminium foil and place them into a warm oven (around 130 degrees Celsius) for 5-10 minutes. Then remove them from the oven and spoon the veggie mixture into them, dividing it equally between the four wraps. Roll up the wraps and serve with your favourite vegan salsa, guacamole or other sauces on the side if desired.

PER SERVING:
CALORIES: 340 | CARBS: 38 G | FAT: 12 G | PROTEIN: 10 G

PERFECT ENCHILADAS

Full of the flavours of Mexico and coasted with a rich and delicious spicy tomato sauce, these enchiladas are completely vegan. Ready to serve in only one hour, they are also perfect for getting the kids involved with the cooking process.

Time: 60 minutes | Serves: 6

INGREDIENTS:

For the sauce:
- 700 g tomato passata
- 1 tsp garlic powder
- 2 chipotle peppers in adobo sauce
- 200 ml water
- ¼ tsp freshly ground black pepper
- 1 tbsp soft brown sugar
- ½ tsp sea salt

For the enchiladas:
- 450 g firm tofu
- 12 tortilla wraps
- 400 g tinned black beans, drained, rinsed and dried
- 1 red bell pepper, de-seeded and stalk removed, finely diced
- 1 red onion, finely diced
- 2 jalapeno peppers, stalk removed, de-seeded and finely sliced
- ¼ tsp cayenne pepper powder
- ½ tsp turmeric powder
- ½ tsp freshly ground black pepper
- ½ tsp sea salt
- 2 tbsp olive oil
- 280 frozen spinach
- 200 g vegan cheese

METHOD:

1. Start by preparing your enchilada sauce. Place the passata, garlic powder, water, salt, pepper, brown sugar and chipotle peppers in a saucepan and add in 1 tbsp of the sauce from the can of chipotle peppers. Turn the heat to medium-high and bring the mixture to a simmer before lowering the heat.
2. Cover the saucepan and leave the sauce to simmer for 10 minutes until it has thickened. Remove it from the heat and allow it to cool.
3. When the sauce has cooled, pour it into a blender and blitz until it is perfectly smooth.
4. Meanwhile, preheat the oven to 180 degrees Celsius and grease a large lasagne dish with olive oil.
5. Put the tofu pieces into a blender and blitz until it turns into a puree. Add in the turmeric, black pepper, salt and cayenne pepper. Blitz again and ensure that all the ingredients are fully combined.
6. In a large frying pan, heat 2 tbsp of olive oil over a medium heat. Then, add in the onion, red pepper and the jalapenos. Leave it to cook for around 5 minutes until the veggies start to brown. Pour in the tofu mixture and stir it through the vegetables, allowing it to cook for a further 5 minutes.
7. Next, place pieces of the frozen spinach into the pan and stir them in, cooking for a few more minutes until everything is cooked through.
8. While the veggies and tofu are cooking, wrap the tortilla wraps in foil and place them into the oven for 2 minutes to warm them. Remove them and divide the filling equally between each wrap. When you have filled a wrap, roll it and set it aside.
9. Pour some of your enchilada sauce into the lasagne dish and place the rolled wraps on the top of it. Ensure that the rolled tortillas are tightly packed together. Pour the rest of the sauce over the top so they are fully covered.
10. Grate the vegan cheese over the top and place the enchiladas into the oven to bake for 15-20 minutes. Remove them from the oven and serve piping hot.

PER SERVING:
CALORIES: 520 | CARBS: 48 G | FAT: 30 G | PROTEIN: 17 G

EASY VEGAN RAMEN

Ready in under 30 minutes, easy vegan ramen is a great dish for families and students alike. You can even allow it to cool and take it to work with you in a flash to reheat during your lunch break in the office microwave.

Time: 30 minutes | Serves: 4

INGREDIENTS:

- 200 g ramen noodles
- 4 cloves of garlic, minced
- 2 heads of Pak Choi, cut into quarters
- 400 g firm tofu, cubed
- 1 large piece of ginger, thinly sliced
- 30 g dried shitake mushrooms
- 4 tbsp soy sauce
- 2 tbsp tahini paste
- 3 tbsp white miso paste
- 2 L vegetarian stock, prepared with 4 vegan stock cubes
- 2 tbsp cornflour
- 4 spring onions, thinly sliced
- 2 tbsp sunflower oil
- 50 g beansprouts
- 2 carrots, peeled and sliced thinly

METHOD:

1. To a large saucepan add the mushrooms, vegetable stock, soy sauce, ginger, tahini paste and garlic. Bring the mixture to a simmer and cover the pan. Leave it to simmer for 5-10 minutes until the ginger has softened.

2. Remove the pan from the heat and strain the mixture through a fine sieve into a clean large saucepan. Discard the contents of the sieve and set the pan containing the broth aside.

3. Heat the sunflower oil in a large frying pan. Place the cornflour in a clean bowl and toss the tofu in it, ensuring it is fully coated. Then remove the tofu from the cornflour and fry it in the hot oil. Fry for 3-4 minutes on each side, turning when it starts to brown.

4. Meanwhile, cook the ramen noodles according to the instructions on the pack, as different brands require varying lengths of cooking time. When they are cooked through, drain them and return them to the pan.

5. Return to the broth and place the pak choi and the white parts of the spring onions into it. Heat the broth for 2 minutes to allow the greens to wilt.

6. Divide the ramen noodles between four separate clean soup bowls and then equally divide the broth and vegetables between the bowls too. Place the tofu on the top and garnish with the green sections of the spring onions to finish before serving.

PER SERVING:
CALORIES: 550 | CARBS: 72 G | FAT: 21 G | PROTEIN: 23 G

VEGAN SPAGHETTI BOLOGNESE

Made with vegan mince, this dish is packed full of deep Italian flavours and is ideal for serving to the kids as a meat-free, healthy alternative to traditional Spaghetti Bolognese.

Time: 80 minutes | Serves: 6

INGREDIENTS:

- 2 carrots, peeled and thinly sliced
- 1 white onion, diced
- 2 celery sticks, finely sliced
- 250 g portobello mushrooms, thinly sliced
- 250 g chestnut mushrooms, sliced
- 2 x 400 g tins of whole plum tomatoes
- 100 ml vegan red wine
- 20 g dried porcini mushrooms
- 4 cloves of garlic, minced
- 1 tsp tomato puree
- 250 g dried green lentils
- 1 tsp soy sauce
- 4 sprigs of thyme
- 1 large handful of fresh basil leaves, roughly chopped
- 540 g dried spaghetti
- 3 tbsp olive oil
- ¼ tsp sea salt

METHOD:

1. Place the dried porcini mushrooms into a large bowl. Boil 400 ml of water and pour it over the mushrooms then set the bowl aside for 10 minutes to allow them to rehydrate.

2. In the meantime, place 1 tbsp of olive oil into a large saucepan. Heat the oil over a medium heat and then add the carrot, onion and celery. Season with ¼ tsp of salt and leave them to cook for 10 minutes, stirring regularly until the veggies have softened.

3. Now, drain the porcini mushrooms but retain the liquid that they were soaked in and set them aside separately. Chop the mushrooms into small pieces.

4. Into the saucepan with the veggies, add the thyme and the garlic. Allow it to cook for a minute before adding in the tomato puree. Cook for a further minute. Then, pour the red wine into the pan and allow the mixture to reduce.

5. Add the lentils, tinned tomatoes and the stock from the porcini mushrooms. Bring the mixture to a boil and then lower the heat. Cover with a lid and leave the mixture to simmer gently.

6. Place 2 tbsp olive oil into a frying pan and warm it over a medium heat. When the oil is sizzling, add in the chestnut mushrooms, portobello mushrooms and the rehydrated porcini mushrooms. Fry the mushrooms until they turn a golden-brown colour. Remove the pan from the heat and pour the mushrooms into the ragu, stirring to ensure everything is combined.

7. Leave the sauce to cook for 35-40 minutes until all the ingredients are fully cooked. You may need to add in a little extra water if the mixture starts to dry out.

8. While the sauce is cooking, cook the spaghetti according to the instructions on the pack. Salt the water before cooking.

9. When you are ready to serve, drain the pasta and set it aside. Remove the sprigs of thyme from the sauce and discard them. Pour the spaghetti into the sauce and stir it through before cooking for a further minute.

10. Remove the pan from the heat and serve. You can garnish with basil or grate some vegan Parmesan cheese over the top for an authentic Italian flavour.

PER SERVING:
CALORIES: 600 | CARBS: 98 G | FAT: 8 G | PROTEIN: 24 G

KATSU CURRY

With its origins in Tokyo, this Japanese curry has become popular across the globe. With tofu as its central ingredient in this vegan version of the dish, it is rich in protein and will give you plenty of healthy energy.

Time: 60 minutes | Serves: 4

INGREDIENTS:

- 2 large white onions, diced
- 2 large carrots, sliced
- 2 cloves of garlic, minced
- 5 tbsp vegetable oil
- 400 g cooked basmati rice
- 1 large cucumber, sliced
- 1 small piece of ginger,
  peeled and finely sliced
- 400 ml tinned coconut milk
- ½ tsp turmeric powder
- 1 tbsp curry powder
- 2 tsp maple syrup
- 1 small handful of mint leaves
- 1 small handful of coriander leaves
- 1 tbsp cornflour
- 300 g firm tofu, cut into large chunks
- 200 g panko breadcrumbs
- Salt and pepper to season
- 1 lime, quartered

METHOD:

1. Pour 1 tbsp of oil into a large saucepan or stockpot and heat it until it sizzles. Add in the onions and the carrots and allow the onions to soften and caramelise. After 8-10 minutes of cooking, add the ginger and garlic and allow them to cook for 30-40 seconds.

2. Stir the turmeric and curry powder into the veg and give them a minute to cook through. Next, pour in 100 ml of water, the maple syrup and the tin of coconut milk.

3. Add salt and pepper to taste, stir thoroughly and cover the pan. Leave the sauce to simmer for 20 minutes over a medium-low heat.

4. Meanwhile, place the cornflour into a large, clean bow and add in 60 ml of water and a dash of salt and pepper. Plunge the tofu into the batter and ensure that it is fully coated.

5. Pour the panko breadcrumbs into a separate bowl and dip the tofu into the bowl. The sticky batter should allow the breadcrumbs to stick to the outside of the tofu pieces.

6. Return to the veggies and remove them from the heat when the carrots and onions have fully softened. Allow them to cool a little before pouring the mixture into a blender. Pulse the mixture to puree it.

7. Next, heat the oil in a large frying pan and fry the tofu pieces for 4 minutes on each side. When the tofu turns a golden shade of brown remove the pan from the heat.

8. Warm up the cooked basmati rice in the microwave and divide it equally between your serving bowls. Top it with the pureed veggies and the tofu. Garnish the bowls with the cucumber slices, mint and coriander leaves and a wedge of lime.

PER SERVING:
CALORIES: 750 | CARBS: 80 G | FAT: 30 G | PROTEIN: 30 G

BUTTERNUT SQUASH CHILLI

A healthy chilli with all the authentic flavours of Mexico. With a mildly spicy undertone and rich taste, this is a perfect meal for al fresco summer dining and equally great as comfort food on a cold winter's evening.

Time: 90 minutes | Serves: 4

INGREDIENTS:

- 600 g butternut squash, peeled and cubed
- 600 g tomatoes
- 400 g tin of black beans, drained, rinsed and dried
- 2 white onions, diced
- 2 cloves of garlic, minced
- 2 tbsp olive oil
- 1 tsp dried oregano
- 1 tsp cayenne powder
- 15 olives, pitted and finely chopped
- 1 vegan-friendly vegetable stock cube
- 150 ml vegan red wine
- 1 handful of chives, cut into small pieces
- 2 Romano peppers, roasted and chopped
- 175 ml vegan sour cream
- 1 bay leaf
- 2 tbsp olive oil
- 1 red chilli, seeds removed and chopped
- Salt and pepper to season
- 400 g cooked white rice

METHOD:

1. Start by blanching your tomatoes. Place them in a large bowl and cover them with boiling water. Leave them for one minute and then remove them from the water. Peel away the skins and dice them.
2. Next, place the olive oil in a large saucepan or stockpot and tip the onions into the pan. Fry them until they soften and turn translucent. Then, add in the garlic and cook for a further 2 minutes.
3. Sprinkle in the cayenne and the oregano and add in the chopped chilli. Add the bay leaf and stir thoroughly. Fry the mixture for 1 minute and then add 200 ml of water and the tomatoes.
4. Crumble the vegan stock cube and add it into the pan, stirring it through. Bring the mixture to a rolling simmer and then cover the pan. Leave it to cook for 30-35 minutes, stirring every few minutes.
5. Uncover the pan and add in the peppers. Season with a dash of salt and freshly ground black pepper. If the chilli is starting to dry out, add in a splash of water.
6. Recover the pan and cook for another 30 minutes, allowing the squash to soften and become tender.
7. Finally, add the beans into the chilli and cook for another 5 minutes. Fish the bay leaf out of the chilli and discard it. Then, remove the pan from the heat and serve with rice, vegan sour cream and homemade guacamole on the side.

PER SERVING:
CALORIES: 380 | CARBS: 32 G | FAT: 16 G | PROTEIN: 10 G

PASTA PRIMAVERA

Packed with an array of delicious veggies, this pasta is reminiscent of an Italian dining experience in Spring. The dish actually originated in New York in the 1970s but it is still full of delicious Italian flavourings that can make you feel like you're in the heart of Tuscany.

Time: 25 minutes | Serves: 4

INGREDIENTS:

- 240 g spaghetti
- 2 portobello mushrooms, sliced and stalks removed
- 225 g asparagus, chopped into halves
- 85 g baby spinach
- 4 cloves of garlic, minced
- 300 g broccoli florets
- 280 g frozen peas
- 1 tbsp soy sauce
- 1 tsp Dijon mustard
- 6 tbsp olive oil
- 2 tbsp lemon juice
- 2 tsp dried oregano

METHOD:

1. Place the spaghetti into a large saucepan filled with boiling water. Add a pinch of salt to the water.
2. While the pasta is cooking, place 2 tbsp of olive oil into a large frying pan and turn the heat up to medium-high. Toss the mushrooms into the pan and fry them for 2 minutes. Sprinkle in the soy sauce and cook for a further minute, stirring the mixture to ensure it doesn't stick.
3. Add the broccoli florets and the asparagus to the pan and cook for another 3-4 minutes, continuing to stir the veggies. Then, add in the spinach and cook for another minute.
4. Add in the peas and the garlic and fry for two more minutes.
5. Remove the pasta from the heat and drain it before returning it to the pan. Drizzle 2 tbsp of olive oil over the spaghetti and toss it well.
6. Transfer the spaghetti to the sauce to finish cooking for the final 2 minutes.
7. While the pasta is finishing cooking, take a small bowl and add in the onion powder, 2 tbsp of olive oil, Dijon mustard, oregano and lemon juice. Add the mixture to the pan and stir it through, ensuring that it is evenly distributed.
8. Remove the pan from the heat and serve piping hot.

PER SERVING:
CALORIES: 410 | CARBS: 57 G | FAT: 15 G | PROTEIN: 14 G

LOUISIANA-STYLE JAMBALAYA

With Cajun flavours, this vegan jambalaya brings the stunning tastes of Louisiana to life. It is a great dinner party favourite that will impress your guests. As a bonus, this recipe is rich in a variety of nutrients, including fibre, Vitamin C and iron.

Time: 45 minutes | Serves: 4

INGREDIENTS:

- 2 large white onions, finely diced
- 4 cloves of garlic, minced
- 8 celery sticks, thinly sliced
- 2 x 400 g tin of chopped tomatoes
- 2 x 400 g tin of butter beans, drained, rinsed and dried
- 2 yellow peppers, stalk and seeds removed and diced

- 1 tsp dried oregano
- 1 tsp chilli flakes
- 4 tsp smoked paprika
- 1 vegan stock cube, crumbled
- 1 handful of parsley, finely chopped
- 60 ml olive oil
- 230 g basmati rice

METHOD:

1. Pour the olive oil into a large stockpot and heat it over a high heat. Add in the onion, celery and pepper. Fry the veggies for 5 minutes until they begin to soften and turn golden.

2. Add in the oregano, chilli flakes, smoked paprika, and tinned tomatoes. Add 400 ml of water and the rice and stir. Next, stir the garlic, butter beans and crumbled stock cube into the pan.

3. Allow the mixture to come to a simmer and then cover the pan. Leave it to cook for 25-30 minutes, stirring occasionally. Keep a close watch on the pan to ensure that the liquid does not fully evaporate because that could cause the food to burn.

4. When the rice is fully cooked, remove the pan from the heat. Sprinkle the parsley over the top and serve.

PER SERVING:
CALORIES: 560 | CARBS: 80 G | FAT: 16 G | PROTEIN: 18 G

VEGETABLE KORMA

This mild, creamy vegan curry is rich and luxurious. Its sumptuous texture and deep spices will remind you of your favourite flavours from the Indian subcontinent.

Time: 40 minutes | Serves: 4

INGREDIENTS:

- 150 g cauliflower florets
- 1 large carrot, peeled and thinly sliced
- 200 g button mushrooms, halved
- 100 g frozen peas
- 2 medium potatoes, peeled and cubed
- 1 large white onion, diced
- 4 cloves of garlic, minced
- 1 small piece of ginger, peeled and finely chopped
- 1 tbsp mild curry powder
- 1 tbsp garam masala
- 150 g passata
- 1 tbsp tomato puree
- 1 ½ tsp cardamom
- 1 ½ tsp coriander
- 1 ½ tsp turmeric
- 1 ½ tsp cumin
- ½ tsp fennel
- ½ tsp fenugreek
- ½ tsp ground cloves
- ½ tsp chilli powder
- ½ tsp sea salt
- 2 tbsp lemon juice
- 120 g vegan yoghurt
- 75 g cashew nuts
- 1 tbsp soft brown sugar
- 400 ml tinned coconut milk
- 1 tbsp coconut oil
- 500 g cooked basmati rice

METHOD:

1. Place the potatoes into a large saucepan and cover them with boiling water. Boil them for 5 minutes then add in the cauliflower, mushrooms, peas and carrots. Boil for a further 5 minutes and then remove the pan from the heat. Drain the water from the veggies and return them to the pan. Set the pan aside for later.

2. Meanwhile, heat the coconut oil in a stockpot or a large saucepan. Put the onion in the pan and cook it until it softens and turns translucent. Add in the garlic and the ginger and fry for a further 2 minutes.

3. While the sauce is starting to cook, cook your rice according to the instructions on the pack.

4. Remove the pan containing the sauce from the stove and add in the tomato puree. Next, add in the mild curry powder, garam masala, cardamom, coriander, turmeric, cumin, fennel, fenugreek, ground cloves and chilli powder. Season with salt. Cook for 2-3 minutes, then add in the passata, coconut milk, cashews and lemon juice. Pour in 300 ml of water and bring the mixture to a boil for 5-6 minutes until the nuts have softened.

5. Remove the pan from the heat and transfer the curry sauce to a blender, blitzing it until it is smooth. Alternatively, use a hand blender to blend it in the pan.

6. Finally, stir the yoghurt into the sauce and sprinkle the brown sugar over. Add a little more salt if necessary. Stir the curry sauce thoroughly.

7. Plate up your rice and ladle the curry sauce onto the top then serve hot.

PER SERVING:
CALORIES: 650 | CARBS: 78 G | FAT: 32 G | PROTEIN: 20 G

RICE AND BEAN BURRITOS

Meaning "little donkey" in Spanish, the classic burrito has been adapted for vegan diets in this exceptional recipe. Filled with rice, beans and other delicious ingredients, it is a quick and easy meal to put together at the end of a long day.

Time: 40 minutes | Serves: 4

INGREDIENTS:

- 4 tortilla wraps
- 1 avocado, finely sliced
- 20 g fresh spinach leaves, roughly torn
- 400 g tin chopped tomatoes
- 400 g tin black beans, drained, rinsed and dried
- 1 clove of garlic, minced
- 1 tbsp chipotle paste
- 1 bunch of coriander, finely chopped
- 1 tbsp olive oil
- 1 lime, juiced and zested
- 250 g white rice, cooked
- 1 red onion, finely diced
- 50 g hazelnuts, finely chopped
- Salt and black pepper to season

METHOD:

1. Heat the olive oil in a large saucepan and add the minced garlic. Allow the garlic to fry for 30—40 seconds before adding the chipotle paste.
2. Pour the tinned tomatoes into the pan and bring the mixture to a simmer. Season the pan with salt and pepper and continue to simmer it until it thickens.
3. Next, add the black beans and cook for a further 3-4 minutes to allow the sauce to reduce. Add the coriander and stir.
4. In the microwave, heat the pre-cooked rice and pour the lime juice over it. Add the raw red onion and hazelnuts and stir thoroughly. Season the rice with salt and freshly ground black pepper to taste.
5. Wrap the tortillas in cling wrap and place them into the microwave for 20-30 seconds to warm them up. Remove them from the microwave and lay them out on a clean, flat surface. Place some of the torn spinach leaves on the top of them, followed by a few slices of avocado. Then, divide the rice equally between each tortilla and finally add the black bean mixture on the top.
6. Roll the burritos by folding up the bottom edge, folding in each side and rolling the wrap upwards to ensure that the filling stays within the wrap.
7. Serve warm with homemade salsa, homemade guacamole and vegan sour cream on the side.

PER SERVING:
CALORIES: 520 | CARBS: 68 G | FAT: 16 G | PROTEIN: 16 G

VEGAN LASAGNE

The ultimate comfort food prepared without meat or any animal products. Smothered with gooey, melted vegan cheese, this vegan lasagne is perfect served with vegan garlic bread on the side too.

Time: 2 hours 30 minutes | Serves: 6

INGREDIENTS:

- 1 large white onion, diced
- 2 celery sticks, finely sliced
- 2 carrots, peeled and thinly sliced
- 4 cloves of garlic, minced
- 30 g dried porcini mushrooms
- 1 tsp tomato puree
- 250 g green lentils, dried
- 250 g portobello mushrooms, sliced
- 250 g chestnut mushrooms, sliced
- 1 tsp soy sauce
- 100 ml vegan red wine
- 90 ml + 3 tbsp olive oil
- 90 g plain flour
- 12 vegan lasagne sheets
- 850 ml soya milk
- 50 g vegan parmesan cheese
- ½ tsp dried basil
- ½ tsp dried oregano
- ½ tsp dried parsley
- ¼ tsp sea salt
- ¼ tsp freshly ground black pepper
- 1 small piece of nutmeg

METHOD:

1. Place the dried porcini mushrooms into a large bowl and cover them with 800 ml of boiling water, ensuring that they are fully submerged. Set them aside for 10-15 minutes to hydrate.

2. In the meantime, pour 45 ml of olive oil into a saucepan and heat the oil over a medium heat on the stove. When the oil is sizzling, add in the onion, celery and carrot. Season with a little sea salt. Cook the veggies for 10 minutes until they soften.

3. Drain the porcini mushrooms but set the stock from them aside to use later. Transfer the mushrooms to a separate bowl.

4. Returning to the vegetables, add the garlic into the pan followed by the dried parsley, basil, black pepper and oregano. Add the tomato puree and then cook the mixture for 2 minutes.

5. Pour the red wine into the pan and allow it to reduce before adding in the dried lentils and the stock from the porcini mushrooms. Bring the liquid to a boil, reduce the heat and cover. Allow the mixture to simmer for 40 minutes.

6. Meanwhile, place 45 ml of olive oil in a clean frying pan and heat it until it starts to sizzle. Add in the chestnut mushrooms, portobello mushrooms and porcini mushrooms. Fry the mushrooms for several minutes until they turn a deep golden shade of brown. Drizzle the soy sauce into the pan and stir thoroughly. Then, transfer the mushroom mixture into the veggie saucepan. Recover the pan and allow it to continue simmering for the rest of the 40 minutes.

7. Turn on the oven and preheat it to 180 degrees Celsius. Grease a lasagne dish with olive oil and set it aside.

8. Pour 3 tbsp of olive oil into a saucepan and sift in the plain flour. Whisk the flour thoroughly and cook for 2-3 minutes. Gradually pour in the soya milk, continually whisking. Allow the mixture to cook for 10 minutes. Grate a little nutmeg into the mixture, adding more or less depending on your tastes.

9. Remove the lentil mixture from the heat and set it aside. Spread around one-third of it over the prepared lasagne dish. Next, add one-third of the white sauce on top of it. Place half the lasagne sheets on the top. Add another third of the lentil mixture and another third of the white sauce and then add the other half of the lasagne sheets. Finally, top with the rest of the lentil mixture and the remaining white sauce. Grate the vegan parmesan cheese onto the top of the lasagne and transfer it to the oven.

10. Leave the lasagne in the oven to bake for 50-60 minutes, keeping a watch on it toward the end of the cooking time to ensure that it does not burn. When the pasta sheets are fully cooked, remove the lasagne from the oven and serve immediately. Pair it with a fresh salad on the side.

PER SERVING:
CALORIES: 550 | CARBS: 64 G | FAT: 16 G | PROTEIN: 28 G

"STEAK" AND ALE PIE

Steak and ale pie is a British pub classic. In this recipe, it receives a vegan makeover. It is a winter favourite and allows you to enjoy a traditional British dish without any animal products involved.

Time: 80 minutes | Serves: 4

INGREDIENTS:

- 1 large carrot, thinly sliced
- 1 celery stick, thinly sliced
- 1 onion, diced
- 2 cloves of garlic, minced
- 80 g frozen peas
- 250 g button mushrooms, halved
- 1 tbsp dark muscovado sugar
- 1 tbsp tomato puree
- 1 tbsp dried thyme
- 2 bay leaves
- 600 g vegan beef-style chunks
- 400 ml dark sweet ale – check that the brand you use is suitable for vegans
- 2 vegan stock cubes crumbled into 100 ml boiled water
- ½ tsp sea salt
- ¼ tsp freshly ground black pepper
- 1 kg frozen vegan puff pastry
- 2 tbsp rice milk
- 4 tbsp olive oil

METHOD:

1. Preheat the oven to 200 degrees Celsius. Grease four medium-sized pie dishes with olive oil and line each dish with a layer of puff pastry. Set some pastry aside to use for the pie lids.

2. Place the olive oil into a large pan and heat it on the stove. Add in the onion and fry for 4-5 minutes until it starts to soften. Add in the carrot, mushrooms and celery. Continue to fry the veggie mixture for another 4-5 minutes.

3. In a separate pan, fry the beef chunks until they are cooked through and then transfer them to the veggie pan. Add in the garlic and cook for another 10 minutes, adding a little more olive oil to the pan if it looks dry.

4. Sprinkle in the dried thyme, place the bay leaves into the pan and add the tomato puree to the pan. Add the sugar and frozen peas and then pour in the ale and the veggie stock. Season with salt and pepper.

5. Bring the liquid to a simmer and cover it. Leave it to simmer for 15 minutes to allow the liquid to reduce. Keep a watch on it to ensure that it does not over thicken or dry out. If it looks too dry, add in some more water or ale.

6. Remove the pan from the heat and carefully fish out the bay leaves, discarding them. Divide the mixture between the four prepared pie dishes. Cut out a round pastry lid for the top of each pie and seal the edges with a fork. Cut a small "X" into the top of each pie with a sharp knife. Brush the lid of the pies with a little rice milk and transfer the pie dishes to the oven.

7. Leave the pies in the oven for 20-25 minutes until they have fully risen and turned golden brown. Then, remove them from the oven and serve immediately.

PER SERVING:
CALORIES: 680 | CARBS: 60 G | FAT: 44 G | PROTEIN: 30 G

RUSTIC VEGGIE CASSEROLE

If you're searching for an easy one-pot dish, this vegan casserole is simple to cook when you require something filling, healthy and tasty to feed your family.

Time: 50 minutes | Serves: 4

INGREDIENTS:

- 200 g carrots, peeled and sliced
- 1 yellow bell pepper, stalk and seeds removed and diced
- 1 red bell pepper, stalk and seeds removed and diced
- 1 large white onion, diced
- 2 celery sticks, thinly sliced
- 800 g tinned whole tomatoes
- 2 courgettes, thinly sliced

- 3 cloves of garlic, peeled and finely sliced
- 250 g cooked red lentils
- ½ tsp cumin powder
- 1 tsp smoked paprika
- 1 tbsp dried thyme
- 1 tbsp olive oil
- 250 ml vegetable stock, prepared with 1 vegan stock cube
- 2 sprigs of thyme

METHOD:

1. In a large saucepan or stockpot, heat the olive oil. When the oil is sizzling, add the onion into the pan and cook it for 10 minutes until the onion softens and begins to brown.
2. Add the celery, red and yellow bell peppers, thyme, cumin, paprika and garlic into the pan and stir thoroughly. Cook the mixture for a further 5 minutes.
3. Pour in the tinned tomatoes and the vegetable stock and stir. Then, add the courgettes and the thyme. Bring the mixture to a gentle simmer. Cover the pot and cook for 25 minutes.
4. Uncover the pan and remove the sprigs of thyme. Add the cooked lentils into the pot and continue to simmer for a few more minutes. Remove the pan from the heat and serve with basmati rice or cooked quinoa.

PER SERVING:
CALORIES: 220 | CARBS: 30 G | FAT: 5 G | PROTEIN: 12 G

MUSHROOM PIZZA

Topped with three kinds of mushrooms and drizzled with chilli oil, this vegan pizza is a delicious flavour experience.

Time: 2 hours | Serves: 4

INGREDIENTS:

For the dough:
- 500 g strong white bread flour
- 1 tsp white caster sugar
- 1 tsp dried yeast
- 2 tbsp olive oil
- 1 tsp sea salt
- 150 ml cold water
- 150 ml boiling water

For the sauce:
- 150 ml tomato passata
- 2 cloves of garlic, minced
- 1 tsp dried basil
- 1 tsp dried oregano
- Salt and freshly ground black pepper to season
- ½ tsp soft brown sugar

For the toppings:
- 100 g portobello mushrooms, sliced
- 100 g chestnut mushrooms, sliced
- 100 g button mushrooms, halved
- 250 g vegan mozzarella cheese, grated
- 1 handful of fresh basil leaves, roughly torn
- 20 ml of chilli oil
- 50 g vegan parmesan, grated

METHOD:

1. To a large, clean bowl add the flour, sugar and yeast. Mix the cold and boiling water together in a large jug and stir. Then, add the olive oil and the sea salt to the jug and stir again.

2. Pour the water into the bowl with the flour and stir it in gradually. Bring the mixture together with a spoon to form a dough and then start to work the dough with your hands. The dough should have a slightly sticky texture.

3. Dust a clean surface with extra flour and transfer the dough to the dusted surface. Knead the dough vigorously for 10 minutes. Then, transfer the dough back to its original bowl and cover the bowl with cling wrap or a clean, damp tea towel. Place the bowl in a warm place to allow it to rise. Leave it for 1 hour until it has doubled in its size.

4. Meanwhile, preheat the oven to 210 degrees Celsius and grease two baking trays. Place the baking trays into the warm oven to heat them.

5. When the dough has risen, remove it from the bowl and return it to the floured surface. Knead again vigorously for several minutes before setting it aside.

6. In the meantime, place the passata, minced garlic, dried basil and dried oregano into a bowl and season with salt and pepper. Add the brown sugar to the mixture and stir well. Leave the sauce to one side while you prepare the pizza bases.

7. Divide the dough into two pieces and shape them into large balls. With a rolling pin, roll each ball into the shape of a pizza base, using extra flour to prevent the dough from sticking if necessary.

8. Remove the warmed baking trays from the oven and dust them with flour. Transfer the pizza bases to the trays.

9. Spread the sauce over the top of each base and then cover each base with the grated vegan mozzarella cheese. Top each base with a handful of each variety of mushroom and add a little extra vegan cheese on the very top.

10. Transfer the pizzas to the oven and leave them to cook for around 12 minutes until the bases have risen a little and the cheese is melted and gooey.

11. Remove the pizzas from the oven, grate some vegan parmesan onto the top, drizzle with chilli oil and top with the basil leaves before serving.

PER SERVING:
CALORIES: 700 | CARBS: 110 G | FAT: 20 G | PROTEIN: 20 G

SEARED AUBERGINE STEAKS

Great served with roast potatoes on the side, these aubergine steaks are flavoursome and tender.

Time: 55 minutes | Serves: 4

INGREDIENTS:

- 4 medium aubergines, peeled and cut into 3 cm thick steaks
- 4 cloves of garlic, minced
- 1 lemon
- 3 tbsp olive oil
- 2 red peppers, stalk and seeds removed and finely sliced
- 4 leeks, finely sliced
- 2 tbsp thyme leaves, roughly chopped
- 2 tbsp tomato puree
- 4 tbsp flaked almonds
- 1 vegan stock cube, crumbled
- 2 tsp apple cider vinegar
- 100 g rocket

METHOD:

1. Preheat the oven to 210 degrees Celsius. Grease a baking tray with olive oil.
2. Place the prepared aubergine steaks onto the baking tray, leaving a small space between each steak.
3. Pour 2 tbsp of the olive oil into a small bowl and add the minced garlic and chopped thyme. Drizzle the mixture evenly over the aubergine steaks, ensuring they are all covered.
4. Place the tray into the oven and bake for 45 minutes, checking regularly to ensure they do not burn.
5. In the meantime, place 1 tbsp of the olive oil into a frying pan and heat it until it sizzles. Add the leeks and the red pepper to the pan and cook for 5-6 minutes until the veggies soften.
6. Add the almonds into the pan and cook for a further 5 minutes. Next, add in the tomato puree, the crumbled stock cube and 75 ml of water. Finally, add the vinegar to the pan. Stir the mixture and cook it until it is hot.
7. Remove the aubergines from the oven and place them on four serving plates. Add the veggies to the plate and serve with roast potatoes or spiced rice on the side.

PER SERVING:
CALORIES: 360 | CARBS: 20 G | FAT: 20 G | PROTEIN: 15 G

PORTUGUESE FEIJOADA

A traditional stew that is popular in both Portugal and Brazil, feijoada is easy to make and is the perfect accompaniment to rice. With black beans as its central ingredient, it is also rich in protein and extremely healthy.

Time: 40 minutes | Serves: 2

INGREDIENTS:

- 2 red onions, diced
- 200 g sweet potatoes, peeled and cubed
- 2 cloves of garlic, minced
- 1 red pepper, stalk and seeds removed and diced
- 1 courgette, thinly sliced
- 200 g tinned black beans, drained, rinsed and dried
- 150 g brown rice
- 50 ml olive oil
- 1 tsp smoked paprika
- 2 tsp coriander, ground
- 4 tomatoes, diced
- 50 g plain vegan yoghurt
- Salt and black pepper to season

METHOD:

1. Pour the rice into a saucepan and cover it with boiling water. Cook it over a medium heat and allow it to come to a boil on the stove. Reduce the heat slightly and leave it to simmer for 15-20 minutes.

2. Drain the rice and season it before setting it aside for later.

3. In the meantime, place the sweet potato cubes into a clean pan and cover the potato with boiling water. Cover it with a lid and cook for 5-10 minutes. Then remove it from the heat and drain the water. Allow the sweet potatoes to steam dry.

4. Heat the olive oil in a large saucepan or stockpot and add in the onions, peppers, courgettes and the cooked sweet potatoes. Fry them for 8-10 minutes

5. Add the black beans to the pan and cook for another 1-2 minutes.

6. Now, add in the paprika, garlic, coriander and a little salt and pepper to season. Cook for 3-4 minutes. Add in the diced tomatoes and 300 ml of water.

7. Bring the mixture to a boil before reducing the heat slightly and simmering for 10 minutes. Allow the vegetables to soften nicely and the sauce to reduce. If the sauce becomes too thick, add in a little extra water.

8. Remove the feijoada from the heat and divide the rice between 2 plates. Divide the feijoada between the two plates and serve.

PER SERVING:
CALORIES: 640 | CARBS: 110 G | FAT: 16 G | PROTEIN: 16 G

VEGAN PAELLA

If you love this Spanish classic but you want your paella free from animal products, this recipe will deliver exactly what you're looking for! Ideal for bringing all the family together to enjoy a fun-filled dinner, paella is a healthy and tasty option that will be popular with both the kids and the adults. This dish includes homemade vegan chorizo too!

Time: 3 hours | Serves: 6

INGREDIENTS:

For the paella:
- 500 g paella rice
- 2 large white onions, diced
- 1 red bell pepper, stalk and seeds removed and finely diced
- 1 green bell pepper, stalk and seeds removed and finely diced
- 1 yellow bell pepper, stalk and seeds removed and finely diced
- 8 tomatoes, cored and halved
- 4 cloves of garlic, minced
- 1 ½ L vegetable stock, prepared with 4 vegan stock cubes
- 700 ml vegan white wine
- ¼ tsp saffron
- 2 tbsp olive oil
- 150 g tofu, roughly crumbled
- 100 g green beans, chopped
- 1 tsp smoked paprika
- 2 tsp paprika
- 1 tsp cayenne pepper
- ¼ tsp sea salt
- ¼ tsp freshly ground black pepper

For the vegan chorizo:
- 30 g plain flour
- 240 g vital wheat gluten
- 30 g nutritional yeast
- 270 ml vegetable stock, prepared with 1 crumbled vegan stock cube
- 110 ml dry sherry
- 1 heaped tbsp tomato puree
- 2 tbsp soy sauce
- 2 tbsp olive oil
- 1 tsp salt
- 1 clove of garlic, minced
- ¼ tsp cayenne powder
- 1 tsp dried oregano
- 2 tbsp paprika
- 1 tbsp smoked paprika
- ½ tsp fennel seeds, finely ground

METHOD:

1. Begin the dish by preparing the vegan chorizo the day before. To a clean, large bowl add the vital wheat gluten, plain flour, nutritional yeast, smoked paprika, paprika, oregano, salt, ground fennel and cayenne pepper. Mix thoroughly before adding the minced garlic, tomato puree, olive oil, soy sauce, sherry and vegetable stock.

2. Use your hands to bring the mixture together and knead it like dough for 5-10 minutes. Remove it from the bowl and cut it into two separate portions. Roll each portion into a sausage shape and wrap each sausage in cling wrap. Then wrap in aluminium foil. Seal each end by twisting the foil firmly.

3. Put the two wrapped sausages into a pan of cold water and place the pan on the stove over a medium heat. Increase the temperature until the water starts to simmer. Leave them simmering in the pan for 1 hour until they firm up. You may need to add extra water to the saucepan during cooking. After 1 hour, drain the water and allow the sausages to cool down. When they are cool, transfer them to the refrigerator and chill them overnight in their wrapping.

4. When you are ready to make the paella the next day, preheat the oven to 180 degrees Celsius.

5. Place a large saucepan or stockpot onto the stove and pour the vegetable stock and vegan white wine into it. Add in the saffron and stir as you bring the liquid to a boil.

6. Pour in the rice and lower to heat. Leave the mixture to simmer for 15-20 minutes, stirring occasionally. You may need to add in a splash of extra water if the pan starts to dry out too much.

7. In a separate saucepan, heat some olive oil. When the oil sizzles, add the peppers and the onion to the pan and season with sea salt. Leave the veggies to cook for 5 minutes until they start to soften.

8. Add in the cayenne, smoked paprika, paprika and garlic and allow the dish to cook for a further 10 minutes.

9. Remove the rice pan from the heat and transfer the rice to the pan with the veggies. Stir thoroughly to combine all of the ingredients. Add in the chopped green beans and the tomato halves. Add in a little extra water and transfer the whole mixture to a large casserole dish. Place the dish into the oven to bake for 30 minutes.

10. Meanwhile, remove the prepared vegan chorizo sausages from the refrigerator. Unwrap it and thickly slice it. Heat some olive oil in a large frying pan and when the oil is sizzling place the chorizo slices and the crumbled tofu into the pan for 4-5 minutes until it turns crispy.

11. Take the paella out of the oven and place the fried chorizo slices and tofu on the top. Serve the paella in the casserole dish as the centrepiece at your dinner table.

PER SERVING:
CALORIES: 615 | CARBS: 55 G | FAT: 30 G | PROTEIN: 22 G

MOROCCAN TAGINE

Vegan, healthy and tasty. What more could you ask for? Rich with flavours that are inherent to North Africa, this tagine is simple to prepare and a joy to eat. Full of nutrient-rich veggies, it is also an excellent source of your essential 5-a-day.

Time: 2 hours | Serves: 6

INGREDIENTS:

- 6 prunes
- 3 carrots. diced
- 5 red onions, diced
- 3 parsnips, diced
- 2 large potatoes, peeled and cubed
- 4 leeks, ends removed and chopped
- 2 sprigs of fresh mint leaves
- 3 cloves of garlic, peeled
- 1 tsp hot chilli powder
- 1 tsp maple syrup
- 1 tbsp cumin powder
- 1 tbsp turmeric powder
- 1 tbsp paprika
- 1 handful of coriander, finely chopped
- 1 small piece of fresh ginger, peeled
- 100 ml lemon juice
- 100 ml + 1 tbsp olive oil

METHOD:

1. Preheat the oven to 200 degrees Celsius.
2. To a blender add 2 of the red onions, garlic, ginger, lemon juice, 100 ml olive oil, maple syrup, paprika, cumin, turmeric, chilli powder and coriander. Blitz the mixture to form a smooth paste. Set the paste aside for later.
3. Pour 1 tbsp of olive oil into a large casserole dish and heat it over a medium heat on the stove. Place the carrots, parsnips, 3 red onions, potatoes and leeks into the dish and cook them for 7-10 minutes.
4. Add the paste you prepared earlier into the dish and stir it through. Next, add in the prunes and stir them in. Add 400 ml of water, cover the dish with a lid and transfer the dish to the oven. Cook for 45 minutes before reducing the heat to 180 degrees Celsius. Cook for a further 45 minutes before removing the dish from the oven.
5. Sprinkle the top of the dish with the chopped mint leaves and serve with rice or thick, crusty bread.

PER SERVING:
CALORIES: 405 | CARBS: 50 G | FAT: 17 G | PROTEIN: 8 G

SPICY VODKA RIGATONI

Popular in the USA, this spicy pasta dish is an indulgent and comforting family feast. With a rich depth of flavour, it is an excellent meal at any time of the year.

Time: 25 minutes | Serves: 4

INGREDIENTS:

- 450 g rigatoni or penne pasta
- 180 ml vegan double cream
- 15 ml vodka
- 2 shallots, very finely diced
- 3 tbsp vegan butter
- 4 cloves of garlic, minced
- 100 g tomato puree
- 100 g vegan parmesan cheese, grated
- 1 tsp chilli flakes
- ½ tsp sea salt
- ¼ tsp freshly ground black pepper

METHOD:

1. Place the pasta into a large pan of salted boiling water and cook it according to the instructions on the pack.
2. In the meantime, place the vegan butter into a saucepan and heat it on the stove. Add in the diced shallots and the garlic when the butter is melted and sizzling hot. Cook for 4-5 minutes to allow the shallots to soften.
3. Add the tomato puree and the chilli flakes and stir. Cook for 4 minutes before pouring in the vodka. Allow the mixture to cook for a further 3 minutes until it has reduced.
4. Lower the heat and pour in the vegan cream, allowing the sauce to simmer for 3 minutes. Finally, add in 50 g of the grated vegan parmesan cheese and stir the sauce constantly.
5. Drain the pasta and keep 100 ml of the pasta water aside. Place the pasta into the sauce and add in the reserved water. Stir the sauce well until it looks extremely smooth and creamy.
6. Remove the pan from the heat and divide the pasta and sauce between 4 bowls. Top each bowl with an equal amount of the remaining vegan cheese, season with salt and pepper to taste and serve hot.

PER SERVING:
CALORIES: 580 | CARBS: 66 G | FAT: 18 G | PROTEIN: 14 G

THAI RED CURRY

Ready to eat in only 30 minutes, this authentic Thai red curry is mildly spicy and provides an exotic taste adventure for your tastebuds.

Time: 30 minutes | Serves: 6

INGREDIENTS:

- 1 medium white onion, diced
- 2 tbsp olive oil
- 4 cloves of garlic, minced
- 1 red bell pepper, stalks and seeds removed and diced
- 1 yellow bell pepper, stalks and seeds removed and diced
- 150 g broccoli florets
- 150 g cauliflower florets
- 2 carrots, peeled and thinly sliced
- 1 small piece of fresh ginger, finely grated
- 400 ml tinned coconut milk
- 3 tbsp Thai red curry paste
- 120 ml water
- 2 beefsteak tomatoes, diced
- 2 tsp maple syrup
- 1 tbsp lime juice
- 1 tbsp soy sauce
- 220 g white rice
- 1 handful of basil leaves, roughly torn

METHOD:

1. Heat the olive oil in a large pan on a medium heat. Add the onion and cook for 3-4 minutes until it turns translucent. Add the ginger and garlic to the frying pan and cook for a further minute.

2. Meanwhile, place the rice into boiling water and cook according to the instructions on the pack.

3. Return to your sauce and add the peppers, broccoli, cauliflower and carrots to the pan and cook for another 3 minutes, stirring constantly.

4. Next, add in the coconut milk, red curry paste and water. Stir the sauce well and bring it to a simmer. Cover the pan, reduce the heat and leave it to cook for 10 minutes.

5. Uncover the pan and add in the chopped tomatoes, maple syrup and soy sauce. Pour in the lime juice and stir well then remove the pan from the stove.

6. Serve the sauce on top of the rice, dividing the portions equally. Sprinkle with fresh basil and serve.

PER SERVING:
CALORIES: 410 | CARBS: 36 G | FAT: 22 G | PROTEIN: 8 G

CHRISTMAS TOFU TURKEY WITH ALL THE TRIMMINGS

A festive treat for every vegan. This tofu turkey with stuffing is a fun and impressive meal to serve up on Christmas Day. It will wow every guest. The only problem is that there won't be any leftovers for the next day because your guests will not be able to resist a second and third helping!

Time: 120 minutes | Serves: 8

INGREDIENTS:

For the vegan turkey:
- 2 kg extra-firm tofu
- 1 tbsp fresh rosemary, finely chopped
- 1 tbsp fresh thyme, finely chopped
- 2 tbsp fresh sage, finely chopped
- 1 tsp dried marjoram
- 1 tsp nutmeg powder
- 1 vegan vegetable stock cube, crushed to a powder
- 1 tsp ground black pepper
- 2 tsp soy sauce
- 80 ml vegan red wine
- 60 ml balsamic vinegar
- 2 tsp Dijon mustard

For the stuffing:
- 1 loaf of wholemeal bread, left exposed to the air overnight and cut into cubes
- 150 g red lentils, cooked and drained
- 3 tbsp olive oil
- 1 large white onion, diced
- 75 g celery, chopped
- 2 vegan vegetable stock cubes dissolved into 700 ml warm water
- 1 tbsp ground flaxseed
- 40 ml water

- ¾ tsp dried sage
- Salt and pepper to season

METHOD:

1. Add the tofu to a blender and pulse until it is smooth and creamy. If your blender is smaller, you may need to blend it in batches, removing each batch and transferring it to a large bowl.
2. Transfer all the blended tofu to a large bowl and add in the rosemary, thyme, sage, marjoram, nutmeg and the crushed stock cube. Stir thoroughly to ensure all the ingredients are combined well with the tofu.
3. Line a sieve with a muslin cloth and place the tofu inside. Then, press down to remove any moisture from the tofu.
4. Leave the tofu in the sieve, cover with a clean towel, place a weight on the top of it and place in the refrigerator for 4-5 hours.
5. While the tofu is chilling, you can make your stuffing. Preheat your own to 180 degrees Celsius and line a baking tray.
6. In a large frying pan, heat some olive oil and fry the onions and celery pieces until they soften. Season with salt and black pepper.
7. Meanwhile, in a small bowl, mix together the ground flaxseed and 40 ml of water and leave it for 10 minutes to thicken.
8. Put the cubes of bread into a large bowl and add in the cooked onion and celery, lentils, sage, flaxseed mixture and some of the stock cube broth, mixing together well. Add in more of the broth until a moist but not wet texture is achieved.
9. Shape the stuffing into large balls, using your hands, and transfer the stuffing mixture to the baking tray.
10. Remove the tofu from the fridge and uncover. Carefully remove the tofu dome from the sieve, transferring it to a lined and greased baking tray.
11. In another bowl, place the red wine, mustard and balsamic vinegar and whisk to combine.
12. Using a brush, baste the tofu turkey with the red wine mixture, ensuring that it is fully covered with a thick layer.
13. Transfer to the oven for 1 ½ hours, removing and basting it again every 15-20 minutes.

14. When the tofu is halfway through cooking, pop the stuffing mixture into the oven for 45 minutes.
15. When the tofu and stuffing are both ready, remove them from the oven and serve with your favourite sauces and some homemade roast potatoes.

PER SERVING:
CALORIES: 460 | CARBS: 5 G | FAT: 42 G | PROTEIN: 6 G

SIDE DISHES

This varied selection of stunning side dishes perfectly complements your main courses or can be served as a light snack on their own. With delicious healthy options and opulent indulgent choices, you will be able to find the ideal side dish to suit your mood and your meal.

CRISPY BROCCOLI

A pan-fried broccoli dish that is quick and easy to whip up in a hurry.

Time: 20 minutes | Serves: 4

INGREDIENTS:

- 1 head of broccoli, divided into florets
- 2 cloves of garlic, minced
- ½ tsp salt
- ½ tsp ground black pepper
- 1 handful fresh flat-leaf parsley, finely chopped
- 1 tbsp olive oil

METHOD:

1. Bring a saucepan of water to a boil and cook the broccoli for 5 minutes.
2. Drain the water and allow the broccoli to steam dry.
3. Heat olive oil in a frying pan over a medium heat on the stove and add the broccoli to the pan, cooking for 2 minutes.
4. Add the garlic, parsley, salt and pepper to the pan and fry for a further 2 minutes.
5. Remove the pan from the heat and serve.

PER SERVING:
CALORIES: 70 | CARBS: 6 G | FAT: 2 G | PROTEIN: 1 G

HOMEMADE ROAST POTATOES

These delicious vegan roast potatoes are worth waiting for. Crispy on the outside and fluffy on the inside, these roasties are an absolute treat.

Time: 80 minutes | Serves: 4

INGREDIENTS:

- 6 large Maris Piper potatoes, peeled and quartered
- 20 g plain flour
- 100 ml olive oil
- 2 sprigs of rosemary
- 1 sprig of thyme
- 1 handful of flat-leaf parsley, finely chopped
- 1 clove of garlic, minced
- Salt
- Black pepper

METHOD:

1. Preheat the oven to 200 degrees Celsius and pour the olive oil into a large roasting tin, lined with foil. Place the tin in the oven to allow the oil to heat up.
2. Place the potatoes in a saucepan of salted boiling water and allow the potatoes to boil for 10 minutes until they are starting to soften but not falling apart.
3. Drain the potatoes and allow them to steam dry.
4. Toss the potatoes in the plain flour. Remove the roasting tin from the oven and transfer the potatoes into the tin, using utensils to ensure they become fully coated in the oil. Sprinkle with salt and pepper and garlic. Place the sprigs of rosemary and thyme on the top of the potatoes.
5. Put the potatoes into the oven for 15 minutes and allow them to cook.
6. After 15 minutes, remove the tin from the oven and turn the potatoes.
7. Return the potatoes to the oven and allow them to cook for a further 15 minutes.
8. Remove the potatoes from the oven, turn them, sprinkle with the chopped parsley and then return them to the oven for a final 20 minutes.
9. When the potatoes have fully browned, take them out of the oven, season to taste and serve.

PER SERVING:
CALORIES: 320 | CARBS: 34 G | FAT: 12 G | PROTEIN: 2 G

SWEET POTATO FRIES

A great side or tasty snack, these oven-baked healthy treats can be cut thicker or thinner according to your personal tastes.

Time: 60 minutes | Serves: 4

INGREDIENTS:

- 4 large sweet potatoes, cleaned
- 1 tsp medium chilli powder
- 1 tsp ground black pepper
- ½ tsp cumin powder
- ½ tsp salt
- 50 ml olive oil

METHOD:

1. Preheat the oven to 180 degrees Celsius and line and grease a baking tray.
2. Cut the sweet potatoes into fry-shaped slices, to your desired thickness.
3. Transfer the sweet potatoes to a pan of boiling water and cook for 6-7 minutes before draining and allowing them to dry.
4. Toss the fries in olive oil, ensuring they are fully coated and season with cumin powder, chilli powder, black pepper and salt.
5. Spread the fries evenly across the baking tray in one single layer.
6. Place the tray into the oven to cook for 40 minutes, removing the tray to turn the fries halfway during cooking.
7. When the fries are browned and crispy, remove them from the oven and serve.

PER SERVING:
CALORIES: 290 | CARBS: 25 G | FAT: 6 G | PROTEIN: 2 G

VEGAN CAESAR SALAD

This lovely side salad is a great low-calorie side that complements any meal.

Time: 20 minutes | Serves: 6

INGREDIENTS:

For the salad:
- 350 g kale, shredded
- 1 large head of romaine lettuce, shredded
- 50 g cashews
- ½ cucumber, thinly sliced
- ½ tsp garlic powder
- 2 cloves of garlic, thinly sliced
- 200 g tinned chickpeas, drained, rinsed and dried
- 1 tbsp olive oil
- Salt and black pepper to season

For the dressing:
- 70 g raw cashews, pre-soaked
- 60 ml cold water
- ½ tbsp Dijon mustard
- 2 tbsp olive oil
- ½ tsp garlic powder
- 1 tbsp apple cider vinegar
- 1 clove of garlic, minced
- 1 tsp soy sauce
- 2 tsp capers
- Salt and pepper to season

METHOD:

1. Preheat the oven to 180 degrees Celsius and line and grease a baking tray.
2. Lay the chickpeas on the baking tray, ensuring they are spread evenly across the tray.
3. Place the chickpeas in the oven for 10-15 minutes to roast.
4. Meanwhile, in a large salad bowl, layer the kale, lettuce, garlic slices, cashews and cucumber and sprinkle with garlic powder and salt and pepper.
5. Place all the dressing ingredients into a blender and pulse until they form a thick and creamy sauce. Remove from the blender and transfer to a dish.
6. Remove the chickpeas from the oven and toss them into the salad.
7. When you are ready to serve the salad, toss the dressing into it and serve.

PER SERVING:
CALORIES: 210 | CARBS: 16 G | FAT: 7 G | PROTEIN: 8 G

HOMEMADE BEETROOT HUMMUS

Healthy and packed with protein, this easy-to-prepare hummus is a vegan treat that's great served on the side or paired with veggie sticks for a quick and easy snack.

Time: 60 minutes | Serves: 8

INGREDIENTS:

- 800 g tinned chickpeas, drained, rinsed and dried
- 400 g raw beetroot, peeled and with the roots removed
- 2 tbsp lemon juice
- 1 tbsp tahini paste
- 1 tbsp cumin powder

METHOD:

1. In a large pan of boiling water, bring the beetroots to the boil and then simmer for 40 minutes until they have softened.
2. Remove the pan from the heat, drain and allow the beetroot to cool.
3. In a blender, place the chickpeas, cooled beetroots, lemon juice, tahini, and cumin powder and blitz until it forms a thick paste.
4. Remove from the blender and serve with pita bread or sticks of celery and carrot.

PER SERVING:
CALORIES: 110 | CARBS: 16 G | FAT: 3 G | PROTEIN: 6 G

GREEK SALAD

Bring the tastes of Greece to your dinner table with a modern vegan twist.

Time: 20 minutes | Serves: 4

INGREDIENTS:

For the salad:
- 1 small head of romaine lettuce, chopped
- 1 small red onion, sliced into half-rings
- 1 red bell pepper, diced
- 150 g cherry tomatoes, halved
- ½ large cucumber, thinly sliced
- 150 g black olives

For the dressing:
- 30 ml olive oil
- 1 tbsp lemon juice
- 1 tbsp red wine vinegar
- 2 cloves of garlic, minced
- 1 tsp oregano
- Salt and pepper to season

METHOD:

1. In a large salad bowl, layer the romaine lettuce leaves, red onion, bell pepper, tomatoes, cucumber slices and black olives and toss well.
2. In a small bowl, combine all the dressing ingredients and whisk until combined and thick.
3. Before serving, pour the dressing over the salad and toss well.

PER SERVING:
CALORIES: 160 | CARBS: 7 G | FAT: 5 G | PROTEIN: 3 G

VEGAN COLESLAW

This coleslaw is so creamy, you won't even realise it's vegan.

Time: 10 minutes | Serves: 4

INGREDIENTS:

- 200 g red cabbage, chopped
- 200 g white cabbage, chopped
- 1 red onion, sliced
- 2 large carrots, grated

- 2 tsp Dijon mustard
- 2 tbsp lemon juice
- 4 tbsp olive oil

METHOD:

1. In a large bowl, put the red and white cabbage, sliced onion and grated carrots.
2. In a separate bowl, combine the mustard, lemon juice and olive oil, whisking them to ensure they are mixed thoroughly.
3. Add the mustard mixture to the veggies and toss it through before serving.

PER SERVING:
CALORIES: 120 | CARBS: 7 G | FAT: 7 G | PROTEIN: 1 G

GLAZED CARROTS

These sweet carrots with a chilli kick make a sumptuous side. They deliver a rich depth of flavour designed to enhance every meal.

Time: 50 minutes | Serves: 6

INGREDIENTS:

- 1 kg carrots, washed and peeled
- 50 ml maple syrup
- 50 g vegan butter
- 1 clove of garlic, minced
- ½ tsp freshly ground black pepper
- ¼ tsp sea salt
- ¼ tsp chilli powder
- ½ tsp fresh parsley, finely chopped

METHOD:

1. Preheat the oven to 200 degrees Celsius and grease a flat baking tray.
2. Slice the washed and peeled carrots into 4 strips by slicing them lengthways and then chopping each slice into 2 pieces. Try to ensure that the slices are as even as possible in size and width.
3. On the stove, heat the vegan butter in a large frying pan very slowly until it is fully melted and then pour the maple syrup into the pan and stir the mixture to allow it to combine with the butter.
4. Add the minced garlic, black pepper, salt and chilli powder to the pan and cook for around one minute.
5. Place the sliced carrots into the pan and ensure they become fully coated with the mixture. Then, remove the pan from the heat.
6. Transfer the glazed carrots to the prepared baking tray, distributing them evenly over the sheet. Drizzle any remaining mixture over the top of the carrots before placing them into the oven for 20 minutes.
7. Remove the carrots from the oven and transfer them to a preheated medium grill. Leave them under the grill for around 3 minutes, keeping a close eye on them to ensure that they do not burn.
8. Remove the carrots from the grill and transfer them to a serving bowl. Sprinkle them with the chopped parsley before serving.

PER SERVING:
CALORIES: 135 | CARBS: 23 G | FAT: 6 G | PROTEIN: 2 G

SPICED RICE

A healthy brown rice dish with a mildly spicy kick that is excellent on the side of any vegan main dish.

Time: 80 minutes | Serves: 4

INGREDIENTS:

- 300 g brown rice, rinsed
- 400 ml vegetable stock, prepared with 2 vegan stock cubes
- 1 corn cob
- 2 red onions, diced
- 2 sticks of celery, diced
- 2 cloves of garlic, minced
- 25 g cashew nuts
- 2 red bell peppers, stalks and seeds removed and diced
- 250 carrots, sliced
- 400 g tin of whole cherry tomatoes
- 200 g fresh cherry tomatoes, cut into halves
- 400 g tin kidney beans, drained, rinsed and dried
- 4 tbsp olive oil
- 2 tbsp smoked paprika
- 2 tbsp Cajun spices
- 1 tsp chipotle paste
- 1 tbsp vegan red wine vinegar
- 2 spring onions, thinly sliced
- 2 tbsp white caster sugar
- 2 tbsp tomato puree

METHOD:

1. Place the cashew nuts into a saucepan and fry them without using oil over a medium heat until they turn golden. Remove the pan from the heat and set the nuts aside to allow them to cool down.

2. Return the pan to the heat and add in 1 tbsp of olive oil. When the oil is sizzling, place the corn cob into the pan and fry it for 1 minute, turning halfway. The outside of the cob should be slightly charred. Remove the corn cob from the pan and transfer it to a plate for later.

3. Meanwhile, place the carrot slices into the pan and fry them for around 5 minutes. Remove the carrots from the pan and set them aside.

4. Place the remaining olive oil into the pan and heat it until it is sizzling. Place the onions and celery into the pan and fry them for 8-10 minutes until slightly softened. Next, add in the garlic and the bell pepper pieces and fry for a further 5 minutes.

5. Pour the tomato puree, chipotle paste, smoked paprika and Cajun spice mix into the pan and fry for another 1-2 minutes. Add in the fresh cherry tomatoes and cook for a further 2 minutes.

6. Add the tinned tomatoes, kidney beans, vegetable stock, sugar and rice into the pan and stir thoroughly. Ensure that all the ingredients are fully combined.

7. Bring the mixture to a boil and then reduce the heat slightly so the liquid is simmering. Cover the pan with a lid and leave it for 40 minutes to gently simmer. After 20 minutes, uncover the pan and stir the mixture then recover and leave the liquid to be absorbed by the rice.

8. When the rice is almost fully cooked, use a sharp knife to slice the corn off its cob and tip it into the rice. Add in the carrots and stir them through.

9. Remove the pan from the heat and transfer the rice to a large serving dish. Season to taste and scatter the sliced spring onions and cashew nuts over the top to garnish.

PER SERVING:
CALORIES: 450 | CARBS: 70 G | FAT: 12 G | PROTEIN: 12 G

SUMMER CORN ON THE COB

Perfect to tempt the kids into eating their veggies, this vegan treat makes the ideal side dish during any family meal.

Time: 40 minutes | Serves: 4

INGREDIENTS:

- 4 corns on the cob
- 100 g vegan butter
- 1 clove of garlic, minced
- 1 tbsp flat-leaf parsley, finely chopped
- ¼ tsp sea salt
- ¼ tsp freshly ground black pepper

METHOD:

1. Preheat the oven to 190 degrees Celsius and lay out four sheets of aluminium foil.
2. In a bowl, mash together the garlic, butter, parsley, salt and black pepper.
3. Place one corn cob on each sheet of foil and divide the butter mixture between the four corn cobs. Wrap the foil over the top of the cobs and seal at each end.
4. Transfer the foil parcels to a baking tray and place the tray into the preheated oven for 30 minutes, allowing them a little longer if they are not soft and tender after 30 minutes.
5. Remove the corn cobs from the oven and serve piping hot.

PER SERVING:
CALORIES: 280 | CARBS: 17 G | FAT: 23 G | PROTEIN: 4 G

MIDDLE EASTERN SALAD

Bring the exotic tastes of the Middle East to your dinner table with this delicious salad.

Time: 15 minutes | Serves: 6

INGREDIENTS:

- 500 g mixed heritage tomatoes, with cores and seeds removed and finely sliced
- 10 spring onions, finely sliced
- 1 large cucumber, seeds removed and finely sliced
- 400 g tin of chickpeas, drained, rinsed and dried
- 1 small bunch of fresh parsley, roughly chopped
- 1 bunch of fresh basil, roughly chopped
- 1 bunch of mint leaves, finely chopped
- 120 ml lemon juice
- 3 cloves of garlic, minced
- 1 tsp sea salt
- ½ tsp freshly ground black pepper
- 120 ml olive oil

METHOD:

1. In a large salad bowl, place the tomatoes, spring onions, chickpeas, cucumber, basil, parsley and mint and toss thoroughly.
2. Into a separate bowl, pour the lemon juice and add the salt, pepper and garlic. Slowly pour the olive oil into the bowl, constantly whisking until the ingredients are fully combined.
3. Pour the dressing over the salad and toss well before serving.

PER SERVING:
CALORIES: 110 | CARBS: 9 G | FAT: 8 G | PROTEIN: 7 G

(KALE CRISPS)

Extremely easy to prepare and excellent as a side dish or a healthy snack, these kale crisps are also a fantastic addition to a buffet and equally good as an amuse-bouche.

Time: 25 minutes | Serves: 6

INGREDIENTS:

- 150 g kale leaves, stalks removed
- 1 tbsp olive oil
- Salt and black pepper to season

METHOD:

1. Preheat the oven to 140 degrees Celsius and line two large baking trays with baking paper.
2. Prepare the kale by washing and drying it, ensuring that there is no moisture left on the leaves. Break the leaves into smallish pieces and place them into a bowl.
3. Pour the water over the top of the kale and mix it through with your hands, making sure all the leaves are fully coated. Season the kale with salt and pepper.
4. Transfer the kale to the prepared baking trays and spread them evenly across the two trays. Place the trays into the oven for around 20 minutes until they have gone crispy. Do not allow them to blacken or burn.
5. When the kale is cooked, remove it from the oven and set the trays down to allow the kale crisps to fully cool before serving them.

PER SERVING:
CALORIES: 30 | CARBS: 3 G | FAT: 1 G | PROTEIN: 1 G

SPICY SALSA

Salsa is excellent when served on the side of Mexican-inspired dishes. This salsa has a strong spicy kick but you can adjust the spice levels to your taste if you prefer a milder salsa.

Time: 15 minutes | Serves: 8

INGREDIENTS:

- 400 g can of chopped tomatoes
- ½ medium white onion, finely diced
- 1 clove of garlic, chopped
- 1 tbsp lime juice
- 1 tsp dried coriander
- 1 small jalapeño pepper, de-seeded and thinly sliced
- ½ tsp sea salt
- ¼ tsp freshly ground black pepper

METHOD:

1. Remove the tomatoes from the tin and transfer them to a bowl.
2. Drain half of the juice from the bowl, ensuring that a little juice is left so the salsa is not too dry.
3. Place the tomatoes, onion, garlic, jalapeños, lime juice, coriander, black pepper and sea salt in a blender and pulse until the mixture is smooth. Do not allow it to become a puree as it should still be slightly chunky.
4. Remove from the blender and transfer to a bowl to serve.

PER SERVING:
CALORIES: 70 | CARBS: 2 G | FAT: 5 G | PROTEIN: 1 G

GUACAMOLE

This smooth-textured dip is an amazing side dish with citrus undertones.

Time: 15 minutes | Serves: 8

INGREDIENTS:

- 3 large, ripe avocados
- 1 medium red onion, thinly diced
- 1 red chilli, de-seeded and chopped
- 1 ripe tomato
- 2 tbsp lime juice

- ½ tsp lemon juice
- 1 bunch of coriander leaves, finely chopped
- ¼ tsp salt
- ¼ tsp freshly ground black pepper

METHOD:

1. Cut each avocado into halves and then remove the stones. Scoop out the avocado flesh from each piece and place the flesh into a blender with the onion, tomato, red chilli, lemon juice and coriander.
2. Gently pulse until the texture of the mixture is smooth but not too runny.
3. Transfer the mixture from the blender to a clean bowl and then thoroughly stir in the lime juice.
4. Season with salt and black pepper and stir them through the guacamole before serving.

PER SERVING:
CALORIES: 120 | CARBS: 2 G | FAT: 11 G | PROTEIN: 1 G

OLIVE TAPENADE

Olive tapenade is delicious when served on crackers or bread. It can be used to accompany an array of main courses or simply served before your starter!

Time: 10 minutes | Serves: 6-8

INGREDIENTS:

- 160 g pitted Kalamata olives
- 3 cloves of garlic, minced
- 2 tbsp capers
- 1 tbsp lemon juice
- ½ tsp dried oregano
- 1 tsp vegan red wine vinegar
- 2 tbsp fresh flat-leaf parsley, finely chopped
- ¼ tsp sea salt
- ¼ tsp freshly ground black pepper

METHOD:

1. Place all the ingredients into a blender and blitz until they form a thick and chunky paste-like mixture.
2. Remove from the blender and transfer to a side bowl.
3. Serve on crackers, pitta bread or mini toasts.

PER SERVING:
CALORIES: 95 | CARBS: 8 G | FAT: 11 G | PROTEIN: 3 G

DESSERTS

Following a vegan diet does not mean missing out on sweet treats. This eclectic selection of vegan desserts is designed to deliver something for everyone. From fruity classics to vegan chocolate delights, you might find it difficult to pick a favourite as they're all so good!

VEGAN ICE CREAM

A creamy vegan vanilla ice cream that can be made with or without an ice cream maker. You won't even notice that it is completely dairy-free!

Time: 40 minutes + freezing time | Serves: 10

INGREDIENTS:

- 240 ml coconut milk
- 270 ml cold water
- 60 ml cold water
- 150 g cashews
- 200 g caster sugar
- 100 g raw, food-grade cocoa butter
- 50 ml coconut oil, melted
- 2 tsp vanilla extract
- 1 tsp salt

METHOD:

1. Place the cashew nuts into a large bowl and pour over the freshly boiled water, submerging the nuts completely.
2. Cover the bowl with a clean cloth and allow them to soak for 2 hours before draining.
3. Transfer the nuts to a blender and add in 270 ml of cold water and blitz until you achieve a smooth texture similar to that of milk.
4. Pour the mixture into a large bowl and add in the coconut milk.
5. Meanwhile, add 60 ml of cold water to a saucepan and pour in your caster sugar. Combine the water and sugar over a low heat and mix them together with a wooden spoon, allowing the sugar to fully dissolve.
6. Then, add in the cocoa butter and coconut oil and season it with the salt, stirring gradually to allow all the ingredients to melt and combine.
7. Next, remove the pan from the heat and pour the mixture into the cashew and coconut milk. Stir to ensure that everything is fully combined.
8. Transfer the mixture to a blender and pulse until it is smooth and creamy.
9. At this point, you can either transfer your ice cream batter to an ice cream maker and follow the manufacturer's guidelines or you can transfer it to a freezer-safe tub and place it in the freezer for up to 8 hours, stirring it every hour to prevent the formation of ice crystals.

PER SERVING:
CALORIES: 330 | CARBS: 26 G | FAT: 26 G | PROTEIN: 4 G

TOFU BERRY CHEESECAKE

This delicious faux cheesecake has a crumbly base and rich topping.

Time: 30 minutes | Serves: 6

INGREDIENTS:

- 340 g tofu
- 200 g demerara sugar
- 1 tsp vanilla extract
- 60 ml coconut oil
- 2 tbsp lemon juice
- ¼ tsp salt
- 200 g fresh raspberries
- 150 g walnuts
- 175 g pitted dates

METHOD:

1. Preheat your oven to 170 degrees Celsius and grease a springform cheesecake baking dish.
2. In a blender, blitz the walnuts until they are finely ground but not powdery. Add the dates in and blitz again until you form a dough-like consistency.
3. Remove the dough from the blender and press it down into the cheesecake tin, covering the bottom of the tin and allowing it to slightly curve up at the sides.
4. Next, clean the blender and then place the tofu, sugar, coconut oil, vanilla extract, lemon juice and one-quarter of the raspberries inside. Whizz the mixture until you get a smooth and creamy batter but do not overdo it or it could turn watery.
5. Transfer the "cheesecake" topping onto the top of the base in the baking tin.
6. Place the baking dish into the oven for 30 minutes until the top is slightly browned and the topping is set and then remove it from the oven and allow it to cool.
7. When you are ready to serve, top the cheesecake with the remaining raspberries.

PER SERVING:
CALORIES: 380 | CARBS: 42 G | FAT: 17 G | PROTEIN: 7 G

SUMMER FRUIT SALAD

Full of vitamins and minerals, this fruit salad is as healthy as it is delicious.

Time: 10 minutes | Serves: 4

INGREDIENTS:

- 100 g strawberries
- 100 g raspberries
- 100 g blueberries
- 1 banana, sliced
- 1 pineapple, peeled and cut into chunks
- 200 ml orange juice
- ½ tbsp vanilla extract

METHOD:

1. Thoroughly wash and dry the berries and prepare the banana and pineapple as stated above.
2. Take a large glass bowl and place all the fruit into the bowl, then pour over the orange juice and sprinkle the vanilla extract over the top, then toss the fruit to combine.
3. Cover the bowl and chill for 2-3 hours before serving with fresh vegan cream or vegan vanilla ice cream.

PER SERVING:
CALORIES: 80 | CARBS: 12 G | FAT: 2 G | PROTEIN: 1 G

VEGAN BROWNIES

When you're in the mood for an indulgent treat, these luxurious vegan chocolate brownies are soft and squidgy with a hint of crispiness around the crust.

Time: 50 minutes | Serves: 8

INGREDIENTS:

- 200 g vegan dark chocolate, broken into chunks
- 130 g self-raising flour
- 2 tbsp ground flaxseed
- 90 ml cool water
- 1 tsp instant coffee powder
- 80 ml coconut oil
- 70 g ground almonds
- 50 g cocoa powder
- 250 g caster sugar
- 2 tsp vanilla extract
- ½ baking powder
- ¼ tsp sea salt

METHOD:

1. Preheat the oven to 170 degrees Celsius and grease and line a square baking tin.
2. In a small bowl, combine the flaxseed and cool water and allow it to thicken for ten minutes.
3. Meanwhile, melt the dark chocolate in a bowl either in the microwave or by placing it in a heatproof bowl over a pan of boiling water.
4. Add in the coconut oil, coffee powder, and 4 tbsp cold water. When the mixture is fully melted and combined, remove it from the heat and set it aside, allowing it to cool a little bit.
5. In a separate large bowl, sift in the flour and add the ground almonds, cocoa powder, baking powder and salt.
6. Returning to the chocolate mixture, whisk in the sugar and then add in the flaxseed mix and vanilla, ensuring that everything is well combined.
7. Finally, add in the flour mixture and whisk everything together, checking that there are no clumps or lumps and that your mixture is very smooth and glossy.
8. Transfer the mixture to the prepared baking tin and place it in the centre of the oven for 35-40 minutes.
9. When the brownies are set and firm, but not hard, remove the tin from the oven and allow the brownies to cool in the tin before removing them.
10. Once they are completely cool, you can take the brownies out of the tin and cut them into squares to serve.

PER SERVING:
CALORIES: 320 | CARBS: 32 G | FAT: 12 G | PROTEIN: 4 G

EGGLESS DAIRY-FREE CUPCAKES

Great for kids' parties, picnics or simply an excellent treat to whip up on a rainy afternoon, these vanilla vegan cupcakes with chocolate frosting are the perfect solution to your sweet treat cravings.

Time: 50 minutes | Serves: 12

INGREDIENTS:

For the cupcakes:

- 135 ml almond milk
- 100 g coconut oil
- 100 g golden caster sugar
- 100 g self-raising flour
- ½ tsp baking powder
- ¾ tsp apple cider vinegar

For the frosting:

- 200 g icing sugar
- 50 g cocoa powder
- 120 g vegan margarine
- 1 tsp vanilla extract

METHOD:

1. Preheat the oven to 180 degrees Celsius and place cupcakes liners inside the 12 holes of a special cupcake tray.
2. Pour the almond milk and vinegar into a small bowl, stir the liquid and set it aside for 10 minutes.
3. Meanwhile, add the coconut oil and sugar to a large bowl and whisk it at a low speed using an electric mixer. Add in the vanilla and then pour in the almond milk mixture, whisking continuously as you pour it in.
4. Next, sift the flour and baking powder into the bowl and whisk again until you have a thick, creamy and smooth batter.
5. Spoon the batter into the prepared cupcake cases and place it in the centre of your preheated oven for 20 minutes. Check on the cupcakes to check they are set as they may need an extra 5 minutes.
6. Remove the cakes from the oven and transfer them in their cases to a cooling rack and allow them to cool.
7. While the cakes are cooling, you can make your frosting. Take a large bowl and add in all the frosting ingredients. Using an electric beater, whisk them until you have a smooth and creamy frosting mixture.
8. When the cupcakes are cool, transfer the frosting to a piping bag and, using a circular motion, pipe the frosting onto each cupcake in a spiral shape.
9. You can dust the tops with a little extra icing sugar or cocoa powder or grate some dark chocolate over the top if you want before serving.

PER SERVING:
CALORIES: 280 | CARBS: 34 G | FAT: 12 G | PROTEIN: 2 G

STICKY TOFFEE PUDDING

Possibly one of the most indulgent desserts out there, this vegan sticky toffee pudding pairs rich sponge with an opulent toffee sauce that will simply knock your socks off.

Time: 40 minutes | Serves: 4

INGREDIENTS:

For the pudding:
- 250 ml soya milk
- 200 g pitted dates, chopped into pieces
- 120 g vegan margarine
- 120 g brown sugar
- 100 ml cool water
- 1 tsp bicarbonate of soda
- 200 g self-raising flour
- 1 tsp vanilla extract
- ½ tsp ginger powder
- ½ tsp cinnamon powder
- ¼ tsp nutmeg powder

For the sauce:
- 220 ml soya cream
- 80 g vegan margarine
- 150 g dark muscovado sugar
- 70 g caster sugar
- 2 tsp vanilla extract

METHOD:

1. Preheat the oven to 190 degrees Celsius and grease and line a baking tin.
2. Pour the water into a large saucepan and add in the dates and soya milk. Bring the mixture to a boil and then turn down the heat and simmer it for 2-3 minutes, allowing the dates to fully soften.
3. Sprinkle the bicarbonate of soda into the mixture and then remove the pan from the heat. The mixture will briefly turn foamy and then darken. Set it aside to cool down.
4. When it has slightly cooled, pour the mixture into a blender and pulse it until the batter becomes smooth but not too loose.
5. Meanwhile, in a large bowl, combine the sugar, margarine and vanilla and beat it with an electric mixer. When it is smooth and light, whisk in the date mixture.
6. Sift the flour, nutmeg, cinnamon and ginger into the bowl and whisk again.
7. Pour the mixture into the pre-prepared baking tin and transfer the tin to your preheated oven, baking for around 25 minutes, until the pudding is fully set but not overcooked.
8. While your pudding is in the oven, melt the margarine for the sauce in a saucepan over a low heat.
9. Add the muscovado sugar and caster sugars to the pan and stir in, allowing them to melt and dissolve with the margarine for 3-4 minutes.
10. Remove the pan from the heat and stir in the soya cream and vanilla with a wooden spoon, ensuring that the mixture turns creamy and does not have any lumps or burnt bits at the bottom of the pan.
11. When your pudding is cooked, remove it from the oven, transfer it to serving dishes and pour the sauce over the top.
12. The pudding can also be served with vegan ice cream or extra soya cream on the top.

PER SERVING:
CALORIES: 460 | CARBS: 38 G | FAT: 29 G | PROTEIN: 2 G

VEGAN TRIFLE

This boozy, rich dessert is great for Christmas Day or any other time of the year and is served in individual glasses.

Time: 35 minutes | Serves: 8

INGREDIENTS:

For the sponge:
- 270 ml almond milk
- 200 g coconut oil
- 200 g golden caster sugar
- 200 g self-raising flour
- 1 tsp baking powder
- 1 ½ tsp apple cider vinegar

For the custard:
- 500 ml almond milk
- 25 g cornflour
- 80 g white caster sugar
- 1 tbsp vanilla extract

For the trifle:
- 100 g strawberries, hulled and halved
- 100 g fresh raspberries
- 100 g blueberries
- 100 g blackberries
- 2 large bananas
- 150 g cherry jam
- The eggless sponge, prepared as above and cooled
- Vegan custard, prepared as above and cooled
- 5 tbsp caster sugar
- 400 ml vegan dairy-free whipping cream
- 3 tbsp sherry

- 50 g vegan dark chocolate, grated

METHOD:

1. Firstly, prepare your sponge by preheating the oven to 180 degrees Celsius and greasing and lining a baking tin.
2. In a small bowl, mix together the almond milk and vinegar and leave it to thicken for 5-10 minutes.
3. In a separate large bowl, beat together the coconut oil and sugar with an electric whisk. Add in the vanilla and the almond milk mixture continuing to whisk while you pour in the milk.
4. Sieve the flour and baking powder into the bowl and whisk again, ensuring that your batter is smooth and creamy.
5. Pour the batter into the prepared baking tin and transfer it to the oven to bake for 20-25 minutes.
6. While your cake is baking, prepare the custard by adding all the custard ingredients to a blender and pulsing until the mixture is smooth.
7. Transfer the custard mixture from the blender to a saucepan and heat it through for 10 minutes, stirring constantly and allowing it to thicken a little.
8. When it reaches the desired consistency, remove the pan from the heat and allow it to cool.
9. Then, when your cake is ready, also remove that from the oven and allow it to cool down on a cooling rack.
10. Meanwhile, mix the berries and jam in a large bowl and then transfer it to the dish in which you will be serving your trifle.
11. Cut the cooled cake into chunks and place them on top of the fruit.
12. Spoon the cooled custard on top of the fruit and cake and smooth the top with a spatula.
13. In a separate bowl, add the vegan cream, sherry and sugar and beat with an electric mixture until it becomes creamy and thickened. Transfer to the top of the trifle.
14. Decorate with grated dark vegan chocolate and serve.

PER SERVING:
CALORIES: 550 | CARBS: 36 G | FAT: 24 G | PROTEIN: 3 G

CHOCOLATE CHIP COOKIES

These sweet treats make the perfect dessert for a dinner party, garden party or picnic and can be wrapped up and taken to work or school as a tasty lunchtime snack. Rich yet light, they are thoroughly fantastic.

Time: 50 minutes | Serves: 10

INGREDIENTS:

- 170 g dark brown sugar
- 100 g white caster sugar
- 190 g plain flour
- 120 g coconut oil, melted
- 60 ml almond milk
- ½ tsp bicarbonate of soda
- 1 tsp salt
- 1 tsp vanilla extract
- 230 g vegan dark chocolate chips

METHOD:

1. Preheat the oven to 175 degrees Celsius and grease and line a baking tray.
2. Place the brown sugar, caster sugar, coconut oil and salt into a large bowl and whisk them together until they are thoroughly combined.
3. Mix in the almond milk and the vanilla extract with an electric whisk until the batter is creamy and smooth and all the sugar has fully dissolved into the batter.
4. Sieve the flour into the mixture followed by the bicarbonate of soda and fold them through the batter.
5. Add the chocolate chips and gently stir them in, making sure they are evenly distributed.
6. Using an ice cream scoop or a large spoon, transfer scoops of the batter to the prepared baking tray. Leave a gap of 5 cm between each scoop as the cookies will spread during baking
7. Place the baking tray into the oven and leave them to bake for 12 minutes until they are starting to turn golden brown.
8. Remove the baking tray from the oven and transfer the cookies to a cooling rack to cool down before serving.

PER SERVING:
CALORIES: 330 | CARBS: 36 G | FAT: 18 G | PROTEIN: 3 G

VICTORIA SPONGE CAKE

If you thought a vegan diet meant you needed to give up some of the most timeless classics on the dessert menu, try this recipe for a classic Victoria sponge cake. Eggless and dairy-free, it tastes even better than the original.

Time: 55 minutes | Serves: 8

INGREDIENTS:

For the cake:
- 300 g self-raising flour
- 200 g white caster sugar
- 300 ml almond milk
- 1 tbsp apple cider vinegar
- 1 tsp vanilla extract
- 150 g coconut oil
- 1 tsp bicarbonate of soda

For the filling:
- 200 g icing sugar
- 100 g vegan margarine
- 1 heaped tbsp strawberry jam
- ½ tsp vanilla extract

METHOD:

1. Preheat the oven to 180 degrees Celsius and line two round cake tines with baking paper. Grease each tin with coconut oil or vegan margarine.
2. In a small bowl, pour the almond milk and the apple cider vinegar and set aside for 10 minutes until the milk curdles.
3. In a separate large bowl, place the flour, coconut oil, sugar, vanilla and bicarbonate of soda. Next, pour in the milk mixture. Whisk the ingredients together with an electric mixer until the batter is smooth and creamy.
4. Pour the mixture into the preprepared tins, ensuring that you put an equal amount of batter in each tin. Transfer the tins to the preheated oven and allow the cakes to bake for 35 minutes.
5. Remove the cake bases from the oven and allow them to cool in their tins. Then, transfer them to a cooling rack to finish cooling down.
6. Meanwhile, in a large bowl whisk together the vegan margarine, icing sugar and vanilla extract with an electric mixer.
7. Take the cooled sponge bases and spread the jam over one of the bases then spread the buttercream filling over the top of it. Place the other base onto the top.
8. Dust the cake with a little extra icing sugar or cocoa powder before you serve it.

PER SERVING:
CALORIES: 470 | CARBS: 72 G | FAT: 22 G | PROTEIN: 4 G

PEANUT BUTTER BARS

A nutty dessert that won't fail to surprise you with its rich and delectable flavours.

Time: 55 minutes | Serves: 16-20

INGREDIENTS:

- 240 g almond flour
- 150 g smooth peanut butter
- 75 g coconut oil, melted
- 75 ml maple syrup
- ½ tsp sea salt
- 2 tsp vanilla extract

- 170 g vegan dark chocolate chips
- 2 tbsp cocoa powder
- ¼ tsp sea salt
- 10 soft dates, pre-soaked
- 170 g walnuts, chopped
- 2 tbsp water

METHOD:

1. Line a square baking tin with baking paper.
2. In a large clean bowl, add in the peanut butter, maple syrup, coconut oil, ½ tsp salt and vanilla and stir all the ingredients until they are fully combined.
3. Add the almond flour into the bowl and stir again, ensuring there are no lumps.
4. Place the vegan chocolate chips into the bowl and stir them evenly through the batter. Transfer the batter to the prepared baking tin and press it down, ensuring that it is even.
5. Place the baking tin into the freezer for 20 minutes.
6. Meanwhile, place the cocoa powder, walnut and ¼ tsp of sea salt into a blender or food processor and pulse the mixture until it is smooth.
7. Add in the dates and blitz the mixture, gradually adding in the water to loosen it. Pulse until the mixture is fully smooth.
8. Remove the baking tin from the freezer and spread the cocoa mixture over the top then return the tin to the freezer for a further 30 minutes.
9. Remove the tin from the freezer and slice the bars into even portions and store them in the refrigerator until you are ready to serve them.

PER SERVING:
CALORIES: 140 | CARBS: 18 G | FAT: 8 G | PROTEIN: 4 G

BLACK FORREST CAKE

Based on the traditional German recipe, this is a vegan cake that will wow anyone who tastes it. It may be a more work-intensive dessert but it is certainly worth it when you sample this stunning cake. Rich in chocolate and cherry flavours that perfectly complement one another, you may be tempted to have a second (and third) helping. With a beautiful aesthetic, it is the ideal centrepiece to finish off a luxury dinner party and equally suited to a family meal or even a picnic.

Time: 90 minutes | Serves: 8-10

INGREDIENTS:

For the cake base:
- 520 ml dairy-free milk
- 440 g plain flour
- 110 g cocoa powder
- 275 g white caster sugar
- 2 tsp baking powder
- ½ tsp baking soda
- ½ tsp sea salt
- 25 ml espresso coffee
- 175 g vegan butter, melted
- 1 ½ tsp vanilla extract
- 1 tbsp apple cider vinegar

For the filling:
- 400 ml tinned coconut milk, chilled overnight
- 60 ml kirsch
- 75 g icing sugar
- 50 g fresh cherries, pitted and cut into halves
- 75 g cherry jam

For the topping:
- 50 ml dairy-free cream
- 100 g fresh cherries, pitted and halved
- 100 g vegan dark chocolate, divided into two

METHOD:

1. Preheat the oven to 180 degrees Celsius and grease and line two large cake tins.

2. In a large, clean bowl, place the plain flour, cocoa, salt, sugar, baking soda and baking powder. Gently whisk the ingredients together and set the bowl aside for later.

3. In a different bowl, pour in your dairy-free milk, melted vegan butter, espresso, vanilla extract and vinegar. Whisk the mixture together until smooth.

4. Pour the liquid mixture into your dry mixture and stir it together, ensuring there are no lumps and the batter is fully smooth and shiny.

5. Equally divide the batter between the two prepared cake tins, ensuring that there is an even amount in each. Place the tins into the preheated oven to bake for 30 minutes until they are fully set.

6. Remove the cake tins from the oven and allow them to cool down for around 10 minutes. Then, transfer them to a cooling rack and prick the top of each cake half with a fork. Drizzle the cakes with the kirsch, allowing it to soak into the shallow fork holes and then leave the cakes to go cold on the racks.

7. Meanwhile, chop half the vegan dark chocolate. Place the dairy-free vegan cream into a saucepan and transfer it to the stove. Heat it gently over a medium heat until it is lightly starting to boil.

8. Place the chopped chocolate into a bowl and pour the hot cream over it, allowing the chocolate to melt with the heat of the cream. When the chocolate is soft and melting, stir the mixture until it turns glossy and smooth and has a creamy texture. Set it aside to cool and slightly thicken.

9. While the cream and chocolate mixture is cooling, prepare the filling for the cake. Open the tin of coconut milk that has been chilling in the fridge overnight and remove the thicker cream from the top, placing it into a large bowl. Do not add in the watery mixture at the bottom of the tin.

10. Whip the coconut cream with an electric mixer for 3 minutes until it is smooth and fluffy.

11. Add the icing sugar to the bowl and whisk it together with the coconut cream using your electric mixer. Set it aside in the fridge to chill for 30 minutes.

12. In another bowl, mix together the jam and halved cherries to prepare the filling for the cake.

13. When the cake bases are fully cool, place one base on a large serving plate or cake stand. Place the sweetened, whipped coconut cream over the top of the base, ensuring that it is evenly spread.
14. Next, evenly place large spoonfuls of the cherry jam/fresh cherries mixture over the top of the cream and then place the other half of the cake onto the top.
15. Spread the creamy chocolate mixture over the top of the cake and around the sides, ensuring that it is fully covered. Grate the remaining dark chocolate over the top of the cake and arrange the pitted, halved cherries on the top before serving.

PER SERVING:
CALORIES: 525 | CARBS: 43 G | FAT: 38 G | PROTEIN: 5 G

BANOFFEE PIE

If you love bananas, rich toffee and a luxurious biscuit base, this is the recipe for you. Providing a vegan twist on a much-loved classic, you can have your cake and eat it with this stunning pie.

Time: 4 hours | Serves: 6-8

INGREDIENTS:

For the base:
- 250 g vegan digestive biscuits, roughly crushed
- 75 g vegan butter or margarine, melted
- ½ tsp cinnamon

For the topping:
- 50 g soft brown sugar
- 370 g vegan condensed milk
- 55 g vegan butter
- 260 ml dairy-free cream
- 40 g cornflour
- 1 tsp vanilla extract
- 2 bananas, peeled and thickly sliced
- 20 g vegan chocolate, grated

METHOD:

1. Prepare a loose-bottomed cheesecake tin by greasing the bottom and sides with vegan butter.
2. In a large bowl, combine the crushed vegan biscuits, cinnamon and the melted vegan butter. Transfer the mixture to the prepared tin and press it down onto the bottom of the tin and around the sides. Place the tin into the refrigerator for 1-2 hours.
3. Just before removing the tin from the fridge, prepare your caramel. In a large heavy-bottomed saucepan, place the condensed milk, butter and sugar. Gradually add in 5 tbsp of the cream, one at a time and whisk the batter until it looks smooth and shiny.
4. Add the vanilla extract to the pan and warm the mixture over a low heat, taking care that it doesn't burn or split. Slowly bring it to the boil and allow it to remain on the boil for around 5 minutes, constantly stirring.
5. When the mixture has the appearance of caramel, remove it from the heat and set it aside to cool. Take care to ensure that it does not become grainy.
6. Take your base out of the fridge and pour the warm caramel over it. Return the tin to the fridge for a further 1-2 hours until it has fully set.
7. Just before serving, layer the sliced bananas over the top. In a large bowl, use an electric whisk to whip the rest of the dairy-free cream and place it on the top of the bananas. Finally, finish with the grated chocolate scattered over the top.

PER SERVING:
CALORIES: 380 | CARBS: 38 G | FAT: 26 G | PROTEIN: 4 G

APPLE CRUMBLE

This quintessential British dessert receives a vegan makeover in this delicious recipe. Ideal when served with a dollop of vegan ice cream or a generous helping of luxurious vegan pouring cream.

Time: 45 minutes | Serves: 6

INGREDIENTS:

- 500 g apples, peeled and diced
- 100 g plain flour
- 50 g brown sugar
- 25 g vegan butter
- ½ tsp cinnamon
- ¼ tsp ground nutmeg
- 2tbsp lemon juice
- 50ml water

METHOD:

1. Preheat the oven to 180 degrees Celsius and grease an ovenproof bowl with vegan butter.
2. In a large bowl, mix together flour, 20 g of sugar, and salt.
3. Rub the vegan butter into the mixture until it takes on the consistency and appearance of breadcrumbs.
4. In the prepared ovenproof dish, mix together the apples, cinnamon, the rest of the sugar, lemon juice and nutmeg. Pour in the water.
5. Layer the crumble topping over the apple mixture in the heatproof bowl, spreading it evenly over the top.
6. Bake for 10 minutes. Remove the crumble from the oven and cover it with a sheet of aluminium foil then return it to the oven for a further 15 minutes.
7. Remove from oven and allow to cool before.

PER SERVING:
CALORIES: 380 | CARBS: 32G | FAT: 35G | PROTEIN: 4G

Disclaimer

This book contains opinions and ideas of the author and is meant to teach the reader informative and helpful knowledge while due care should be taken by the user in the application of the information provided. The instructions and strategies are possibly not right for every reader and there is no guarantee that they work for everyone. Using this book and implementing the information/recipes therein contained is explicitly your own responsibility and risk. This work with all its contents, does not guarantee correctness, completion, quality or correctness of the provided information. Misinformation or misprints cannot be completely eliminated.

Printed in Great Britain
by Amazon